QuietTime

one year daily devotional for students

GIVE ME
UNDERSTANDING
ACCORDING
TO YOUR WORD

QuietTime
one year daily devotional for students

Word of Life Local Church Ministries
A division of Word of Life Fellowship, Inc.
Joe Jordan – Executive Director
Don Lough – Director
Jack Wyrtzen & Harry Bollback – Founders
Mike Calhoun – VP of Local Church Ministries

USA	Canada
P.O. Box 600	RR#8/Owen Sound
Schroon Lake, NY 12870	ON, Canada N4K 5W4
talk@wol.org	LCM@wol.ca
1-888-932-5827	1-800-461-3503

Web Address: www.wol.org

Publisher's Acknowledgements

Writers and Contributors:

Bobby Barton	Zechariah
Matt Boutilier	Hebrews
Vince Estill	Amos/Obadiah, Jonah/Micah, Joshua, Judges
Cory Fehr	2 Timothy, Titus/Philemon
Paul O'Bradovic	Revelation
Joe and Gloria Phillips	Ephesians, John
Matt Walls	1 Corinthians, Proverbs, Psalms

Editor: Dale Flynn
Curriculum Manager: Don Reichard
Cover and page design: Boire Design

ISBN - 978-1-931235-93-8
Printed in the United States of America

helpful hints for a daily Quiet Time

The purpose of this Quiet Time is to meet the needs of spiritual growth in the life of the Christian in such a way that they learn the art of conducting their own personal investigation into the Bible. Consider the following helpful hints:

1 Give priority in choosing your quiet time. This will vary with each individual in accordance with his own circumstances. The time you choose must:
- have top priority over everything else
- be the quietest time possible.
- be a convenient time of the day or night.
- be consistently observed each day.

2 Give attention to the procedure suggested for you to follow. Include the following items.
- Read God's Word.
- Mark your Bible as you read. Here are some suggestions that might be helpful:
  a. After you read the passage put an exclamation mark next to the verses you completely understand.
  b. Put a question mark next to verses you do not understand.
  c. Put an arrow pointing upward next to encouraging verses.
  d. Put an arrow pointing downward next to verses which weigh us down in our spiritual race.
  e. Put a star next to verses containing important truths or major points.
- Meditate on what you have read (In one sentence, write the main thought). Here are some suggestions as guidelines for meditating on God's Word:
  a. Look at the selected passage from God's point of view.

b. Though we encourage quiet time in the morning, some people arrange to have their quiet time at the end of their day. God emphasizes that we need to go to sleep meditating on His Word. "My soul shall be satisfied and my mouth shall praise thee with joyful lips: when I remember thee upon my bed, and meditating on thee in the night watches" (Psalm 63:5,6).

c. Deuteronomy 6:7 lists routine things you do each day during which you should concentrate on the portion of Scripture for that day:
- — when you sit in your house (meals and relaxation)
- — when you walk in the way (to and from school or work)
- — when you lie down (before going to sleep at night)
- — when you rise up (getting ready for the day)

■ Apply some truth to your life. (Use first person pronouns I, me, my, mine). If you have difficulty in finding an application for your life, think of yourself as a Bible SPECTator and ask yourself the following questions.

S – is there any sin for me to forsake?

P – is there any promise for me to claim?

E – is there any example for me to follow?

C – is there any command for me to obey?

T – is there anything to be thankful for today?

■ Pray for specific things (Use the prayer sheets found in the My Prayer Journal section).

3 Be sure to fill out your quiet time sheets. This will really help you remember the things the Lord brings to your mind.

4 Purpose to share with someone else each day something you gained from your quiet time. This can be a real blessing for them as well as for you.

Step by step through your QuietTime

The Quiet Time for Students will help you have a special time each day with the Lord. The daily passages are organized so that you cover every book of the Bible in six years. All Word of Life quiet times use the same daily passage for all ages, so families, small groups, or even entire churches can encourage each other from the Word of God.

The following instructions walk you through the steps for using the Quiet Time.

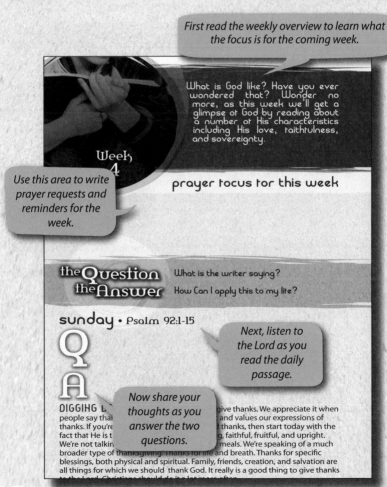

First read the weekly overview to learn what the focus is for the coming week.

What is God like? Have you ever wondered that? Wonder no more, as this week we'll get a glimpse of God by reading about a number of His characteristics including His love, faithfulness, and sovereignty.

Week 4

Use this area to write prayer requests and reminders for the week.

prayer focus for this week

the **Question** the **Answer**

What is the writer saying?

How can I apply this to my life?

sunday · Psalm 92:1-15

Next, listen to the Lord as you read the daily passage.

Q

A

Now share your thoughts as you answer the two questions.

DIGGING D... ...give thanks. We appreciate it when people say tha... ...and values our expressions of thanks. If you're... ...thanks, then start today with the fact that He is t... ...g, faithful, fruitful, and upright. We're not talkin... ...meals. We're speaking of a much broader type of thanksgiving. Thanks for life and breath. Thanks for specific blessings, both physical and spiritual. Family, friends, creation, and salvation are all things for which we should thank God. It really is a good thing to give thanks

5

monday • Psalm 93:1-5

Take time to read the Digging Deeper commentary for additional insights on the text.

DIGGING DEEPER • God is King. There's no doubt about who rules _____ in this universe. It is God and God alone. He has been the King _____ past and will continue to be King forever. The earth and seas _____ e fact that He is King, and all creation agrees as well. As you look _____ is Psalm, you'll notice several characteristics about this King: He _____ omnipotent, immovable, eternal, mighty, and holy. In a phrase, _____ of kings. And because He is King, we owe Him the respect and _____ y other king deserves and much more.

_____ one act before royalty? How can this apply to our relationship with God? How can you honor your King today?

tuesday • Psalm 94:1-11

DIGGING DEEPER • Have you ever questioned authority? Sure you have! At some point in your life you've questioned your parents, teachers, and even pastors. In fact, most of you have probably even questioned the ultimate authority, God Himself. Maybe you've wo _____ godly grandparent to die, or perhaps you _____ diagnosed with cancer. To a certain exter _____ all had those feelings that He wasn't payi _____ The fact of the matter is that God is aware of our problems. H _____ derstands our situation, and His timing is perfect. You can count on H:m.

Consider these questions as you begin your prayer time.

What have you questioned God about in the past? Do you still have some questions?

Use the weekly and daily prayer pages in the front of the Quiet Time to organize your prayer time as God leads you.

my personal
prayer journal

Sunday

family

mom
dad
~~⊘⊘⊘~~

christian friends

Jessica Mac

Jacob

Leah?

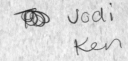 Jodi

Ken

Monday

family

Nana

christian friends

Mary Sue
Coach P
Mr. Davis
Mr. Mann

Clayton Carter
Taylor Dell
Candler

Tuesday

family

Grandpa + Grandma
Melissa
Chrissy
Monica

christian friends

Kayla B

Jenny
Lauren

missionaries

Wednesday

family

Uncle Joe
Aunt Cathy
Kaitlyn + TG
Ben

christian friends

Jaclyn
Matt
Schlegal

Jordan W
Cole

Thursday

family

Aunt D
Uncle M
Tiger

christian friends

Hay Bell
Chels
Sarah

Vordyn Lang

missionaries

friday

family

Uncle Ryan
Aunt Gretchen
Justin
Jamie
Josh
Yaya

christian friends

Mallory

unsaved friends

Brody

missionaries

Tony

Saturday

family

sister

christian friends

Sk

Kimbo
Andrew
meagan
SAM

unsaved friends

missionaries

Praise List

Praise List

Praise List

date/answer

Praise List

Something for Everyone

Some people just can't get enough! That is why we have several dimensions in the Word of Life Quiet Time. Along with the daily reading, content and application questions for each day, two reading programs are given to help you understand the Bible better. Choose one or both.

Reading Through the New Testament Four Times In One Year

Turn the page and discover a schedule that takes you through the New Testament four times in one year. This is a great method to help you see the correlation of the Gospels and other New Testament books.

Reading Through the Whole Bible In One Year

Turn another page and find a program of several pages that will guide you through a chronological reading of the entire Bible. Follow this schedule and you will move from Genesis through Revelation in one year.

The Choice is Up to You

Whether you have a short quiet time, a quiet time with more scripture reading or one with a mini-Bible study each day, we trust your time with God will draw you closer to Him in every area of your life.

Read through the new testament four times in one year

Weeks 1-13

- ☐ Matthew 1-3
- ☐ Matthew 4-6
- ☐ Matthew 7-9
- ☐ Matt. 10-12
- ☐ Matt. 13-15
- ☐ Matt. 16-18
- ☐ Matt. 19-21
- ☐ Matt. 22-24
- ☐ Matt. 25-26
- ☐ Matt. 27-28
- ☐ Mark 1-3
- ☐ Mark 4-5
- ☐ Mark 6-8
- ☐ Mark 9-11
- ☐ Mark 12-14
- ☐ Mark 15-16
- ☐ Luke 1-2
- ☐ Luke 3-5
- ☐ Luke 6-7
- ☐ Luke 8-9
- ☐ Luke 10-11
- ☐ Luke 12-14
- ☐ Luke 15-17
- ☐ Luke 18-20
- ☐ Luke 21-22
- ☐ Luke 23-24
- ☐ John 1-3
- ☐ John 4-5
- ☐ John 6-7
- ☐ John 8-10
- ☐ John 11-12
- ☐ John 13-15
- ☐ John 16-18
- ☐ John 19-21
- ☐ Acts 1-3
- ☐ Acts 4-6
- ☐ Acts 7-8
- ☐ Acts 9-11
- ☐ Acts 12-15
- ☐ Acts 16-18
- ☐ Acts 19-21
- ☐ Acts 22-24
- ☐ Acts 25-26
- ☐ Acts 27-28
- ☐ Romans 1-3

- ☐ Romans 4-6
- ☐ Romans 7-9
- ☐ Romans 10-12
- ☐ Romans 13-16
- ☐ 1 Cor. 1-4
- ☐ 1 Cor. 5-9
- ☐ 1 Cor. 10-12
- ☐ 1 Cor. 13-16
- ☐ 2 Cor. 1-4
- ☐ 2 Cor. 5-8
- ☐ 2 Cor. 9-13
- ☐ Galatians 1-3
- ☐ Galatians 4-6
- ☐ Ephesians 1-3
- ☐ Ephesians 4-6
- ☐ Philippians 1-4
- ☐ Colossians 1-4
- ☐ 1 Thes. 1-3
- ☐ 1 Thes. 4-5
- ☐ 2 Thes. 1-3
- ☐ 1 Timothy 1-3
- ☐ 1 Timothy 4-6
- ☐ 2 Timothy 1-4
- ☐ Titus 1-3
- ☐ Philemon
- ☐ Hebrews 1
- ☐ Hebrews 2-4
- ☐ Hebrews 5-7
- ☐ Hebrews 8-10
- ☐ Hebrews 11-13
- ☐ James 1-3
- ☐ James 4-5
- ☐ 1 Peter 1-3
- ☐ 1 Peter 4-5
- ☐ 2 Peter 1-3
- ☐ 1 John 1-3
- ☐ 1 John 4-5
- ☐ 2 Jn, 3 Jn, Jude
- ☐ Revelation 1-3
- ☐ Revelation 4-6
- ☐ Revelation 7-9
- ☐ Rev. 10-12
- ☐ Rev. 13-15
- ☐ Rev. 16-18
- ☐ Rev. 19-22

Weeks 14-26

- ☐ Matthew 1-3
- ☐ Matthew 4-6
- ☐ Matthew 7-9
- ☐ Matt. 10-12
- ☐ Matt. 13-15
- ☐ Matt. 16-18
- ☐ Matt. 19-21
- ☐ Matt. 22-24
- ☐ Matt. 25-26
- ☐ Matt. 27-28
- ☐ Mark 1-3
- ☐ Mark 4-5
- ☐ Mark 6-8
- ☐ Mark 9-11
- ☐ Mark 12-14
- ☐ Mark 15-16
- ☐ Luke 1-2
- ☐ Luke 3-5
- ☐ Luke 6-7
- ☐ Luke 8-9
- ☐ Luke 10-11
- ☐ Luke 12-14
- ☐ Luke 15-17
- ☐ Luke 18-20
- ☐ Luke 21-22
- ☐ Luke 23-24
- ☐ John 1-3
- ☐ John 4-5
- ☐ John 6-7
- ☐ John 8-10
- ☐ John 11-12
- ☐ John 13-15
- ☐ John 16-18
- ☐ John 19-21
- ☐ Acts 1-3
- ☐ Acts 4-6
- ☐ Acts 7-8
- ☐ Acts 9-11
- ☐ Acts 12-15
- ☐ Acts 16-18
- ☐ Acts 19-21
- ☐ Acts 22-24
- ☐ Acts 25-26
- ☐ Acts 27-28
- ☐ Romans 1-3

- ☐ Romans 4-6
- ☐ Romans 7-9
- ☐ Romans 10-12
- ☐ Romans 13-16
- ☐ 1 Cor. 1-4
- ☐ 1 Cor. 5-9
- ☐ 1 Cor. 10-12
- ☐ 1 Cor. 13-16
- ☐ 2 Cor. 1-4
- ☐ 2 Cor. 5-8
- ☐ 2 Cor. 9-13
- ☐ Galatians 1-3
- ☐ Galatians 4-6
- ☐ Ephesians 1-3
- ☐ Ephesians 4-6
- ☐ Philippians 1-4
- ☐ Colossians 1-4
- ☐ 1 Thes. 1-3
- ☐ 1 Thes. 4-5
- ☐ 2 Thes. 1-3
- ☐ 1 Timothy 1-3
- ☐ 1 Timothy 4-6
- ☐ 2 Timothy 1-4
- ☐ Titus 1-3
- ☐ Philemon
- ☐ Hebrews 1
- ☐ Hebrews 2-4
- ☐ Hebrews 5-7
- ☐ Hebrews 8-10
- ☐ Hebrews 11-13
- ☐ James 1-3
- ☐ James 4-5
- ☐ 1 Peter 1-3
- ☐ 1 Peter 4-5
- ☐ 2 Peter 1-3
- ☐ 1 John 1-3
- ☐ 1 John 4-5
- ☐ 2 Jn, 3 Jn, Jude
- ☐ Revelation 1-3
- ☐ Revelation 4-6
- ☐ Revelation 7-9
- ☐ Rev. 10-12
- ☐ Rev. 13-15
- ☐ Rev. 16-18
- ☐ Rev. 19-22

Read through the new testament four times in one year

Weeks 27-39

- ☐ Matthew 1-3
- ☐ Matthew 4-6
- ☐ Matthew 7-9
- ☐ Matt. 10-12
- ☐ Matt. 13-15
- ☐ Matt. 16-18
- ☐ Matt. 19-21
- ☐ Matt. 22-24
- ☐ Matt. 25-26
- ☐ Matt. 27-28
- ☐ Mark 1-3
- ☐ Mark 4-5
- ☐ Mark 6-8
- ☐ Mark 9-11
- ☐ Mark 12-14
- ☐ Mark 15-16
- ☐ Luke 1-2
- ☐ Luke 3-5
- ☐ Luke 6-7
- ☐ Luke 8-9
- ☐ Luke 10-11
- ☐ Luke 12-14
- ☐ Luke 15-17
- ☐ Luke 18-20
- ☐ Luke 21-22
- ☐ Luke 23-24
- ☐ John 1-3
- ☐ John 4-5
- ☐ John 6-7
- ☐ John 8-10
- ☐ John 11-12
- ☐ John 13-15
- ☐ John 16-18
- ☐ John 19-21
- ☐ Acts 1-3
- ☐ Acts 4-6
- ☐ Acts 7-8
- ☐ Acts 9-11
- ☐ Acts 12-15
- ☐ Acts 16-18
- ☐ Acts 19-21
- ☐ Acts 22-24
- ☐ Acts 25-26
- ☐ Acts 27-28
- ☐ Romans 1-3

- ☐ Romans 4-6
- ☐ Romans 7-9
- ☐ Romans 10-12
- ☐ Romans 13-16
- ☐ 1 Cor. 1-4
- ☐ 1 Cor. 5-9
- ☐ 1 Cor. 10-12
- ☐ 1 Cor. 13-16
- ☐ 2 Cor. 1-4
- ☐ 2 Cor. 5-8
- ☐ 2 Cor. 9-13
- ☐ Galatians 1-3
- ☐ Galatians 4-6
- ☐ Ephesians 1-3
- ☐ Ephesians 4-6
- ☐ Phil. 1-4
- ☐ Colossians 1-4
- ☐ 1 Thes. 1-3
- ☐ 1 Thes. 4-5
- ☐ 2 Thes. 1-3
- ☐ 1 Timothy 1-3
- ☐ 1 Timothy 4-6
- ☐ 2 Timothy 1-4
- ☐ Titus 1-3
- ☐ Philemon
- ☐ Hebrews 1
- ☐ Hebrews 2-4
- ☐ Hebrews 5-7
- ☐ Hebrews 8-10
- ☐ Hebrews 11-13
- ☐ James 1-3
- ☐ James 4-5
- ☐ 1 Peter 1-3
- ☐ 1 Peter 4-5
- ☐ 2 Peter 1-3
- ☐ 1 John 1-3
- ☐ 1 John 4-5
- ☐ 2 Jn, 3 Jn, Jude
- ☐ Revelation 1-3
- ☐ Revelation 4-6
- ☐ Revelation 7-9
- ☐ Rev. 10-12
- ☐ Rev. 13-15
- ☐ Rev. 16-18
- ☐ Rev. 19-22

Weeks 40-52

- ☐ Matthew 1-3
- ☐ Matthew 4-6
- ☐ Matthew 7-9
- ☐ Matt. 10-12
- ☐ Matt. 13-15
- ☐ Matt. 16-18
- ☐ Matt. 19-21
- ☐ Matt. 22-24
- ☐ Matt. 25-26
- ☐ Matt. 27-28
- ☐ Mark 1-3
- ☐ Mark 4-5
- ☐ Mark 6-8
- ☐ Mark 9-11
- ☐ Mark 12-14
- ☐ Mark 15-16
- ☐ Luke 1-2
- ☐ Luke 3-5
- ☐ Luke 6-7
- ☐ Luke 8-9
- ☐ Luke 10-11
- ☐ Luke 12-14
- ☐ Luke 15-17
- ☐ Luke 18-20
- ☐ Luke 21-22
- ☐ Luke 23-24
- ☐ John 1-3
- ☐ John 4-5
- ☐ John 6-7
- ☐ John 8-10
- ☐ John 11-12
- ☐ John 13-15
- ☐ John 16-18
- ☐ John 19-21
- ☐ Acts 1-3
- ☐ Acts 4-6
- ☐ Acts 7-8
- ☐ Acts 9-11
- ☐ Acts 12-15
- ☐ Acts 16-18
- ☐ Acts 19-21
- ☐ Acts 22-24
- ☐ Acts 25-26
- ☐ Acts 27-28
- ☐ Romans 1-3

- ☐ Romans 4-6
- ☐ Romans 7-9
- ☐ Romans 10-12
- ☐ Romans 13-16
- ☐ 1 Cor. 1-4
- ☐ 1 Cor. 5-9
- ☐ 1 Cor. 10-12
- ☐ 1 Cor. 13-16
- ☐ 2 Cor. 1-4
- ☐ 2 Cor. 5-8
- ☐ 2 Cor. 9-13
- ☐ Galatians 1-3
- ☐ Galatians 4-6
- ☐ Ephesians 1-3
- ☐ Ephesians 4-6
- ☐ Phil. 1-4
- ☐ Colossians 1-4
- ☐ 1 Thes. 1-3
- ☐ 1 Thes. 4-5
- ☐ 2 Thes. 1-3
- ☐ 1 Timothy 1-3
- ☐ 1 Timothy 4-6
- ☐ 2 Timothy 1-4
- ☐ Titus 1-3
- ☐ Philemon
- ☐ Hebrews 1
- ☐ Hebrews 2-4
- ☐ Hebrews 5-7
- ☐ Hebrews 8-10
- ☐ Hebrews 11-13
- ☐ James 1-3
- ☐ James 4-5
- ☐ 1 Peter 1-3
- ☐ 1 Peter 4-5
- ☐ 2 Peter 1-3
- ☐ 1 John 1-3
- ☐ 1 John 4-5
- ☐ 2 Jn, 3 Jn, Jude
- ☐ Revelation 1-3
- ☐ Revelation 4-6
- ☐ Revelation 7-9
- ☐ Rev. 10-12
- ☐ Rev. 13-15
- ☐ Rev. 16-18
- ☐ Rev. 19-22

Bible reading schedule

Read through the Bible in one year! As you complete each daily reading, simply place a check in the appropriate box.

☑ 1 Genesis 1-3	☐ 53 Leviticus 18-20
☑ 2 Genesis 4:1-6:8	☐ 54 Leviticus 21-23
☑ 3 Genesis 6:9-9:29	☐ 55 Leviticus 24-25
☑ 4 Genesis 10-11	☐ 56 Leviticus 26-27
☐ 5 Genesis 12-14	☐ 57 Numbers 1-2
☑ 6 Genesis 15-17	☐ 58 Numbers 3-4
☑ 7 Genesis 18-19	☐ 59 Numbers 5-6
☑ 8 Genesis 20-22	☐ 60 Numbers 7
☑ 9 Genesis 23-24	☐ 61 Numbers 8-10
☑ 10 Genesis 25-26	☐ 62 Numbers 11-13
☑ 11 Genesis 27-28	☐ 63 Numbers 14-15
☑ 12 Genesis 29-30	☐ 64 Numbers 16-18
☑ 13 Genesis 31-32	☐ 65 Numbers 19-21
☑ 14 Genesis 33-35	☐ 66 Numbers 22-24
☑ 15 Genesis 36-37	☐ 67 Numbers 25-26
☑ 16 Genesis 38-40	☐ 68 Numbers 27-29
☑ 17 Genesis 41-42	☐ 69 Numbers 30-31
☐ 18 Genesis 43-45	☐ 70 Numbers 32-33
☐ 19 Genesis 46-47	☐ 71 Numbers 34-36
☐ 20 Genesis 48-50	☐ 72 Deuteronomy 1-2
☐ 21 Job 1-3	☐ 73 Deuteronomy 3-4
☐ 22 Job 4-7	☐ 74 Deuteronomy 5-7
☐ 23 Job 8-11	☐ 75 Deuteronomy 8-10
☐ 24 Job 12-15	☐ 76 Deuteronomy 11-13
☐ 25 Job 16-19	☐ 77 Deuteronomy 14-17
☐ 26 Job 20-22	☐ 78 Deuteronomy 18-21
☐ 27 Job 23-28	☐ 79 Deuteronomy 22-25
☐ 28 Job 29-31	☐ 80 Deuteronomy 26-28
☐ 29 Job 32-34	☐ 81 Deuteronomy 29:1-31:29
☐ 30 Job 35-37	☐ 82 Deuteronomy 31:30-34:12
☐ 31 Job 38-42	☐ 83 Joshua 1-4
☐ 32 Exodus 1-4	☐ 84 Joshua 5-8
☐ 33 Exodus 5-8	☐ 85 Joshua 9-11
☐ 34 Exodus 9-11	☐ 86 Joshua 12-14
☐ 35 Exodus 12-13	☐ 87 Joshua 15-17
☐ 36 Exodus 14-15	☐ 88 Joshua 18-19
☐ 37 Exodus 16-18	☐ 89 Joshua 20-22
☐ 38 Exodus 19-21	☐ 90 Joshua 23 - Judges 1
☐ 39 Exodus 22-24	☐ 91 Judges 2-5
☐ 40 Exodus 25-27	☐ 92 Judges 6-8
☐ 41 Exodus 28-29	☐ 93 Judges 9
☐ 42 Exodus 30-31	☐ 94 Judges 10-12
☐ 43 Exodus 32-34	☐ 95 Judges 13-16
☐ 44 Exodus 35-36	☐ 96 Judges 17-19
☐ 45 Exodus 37-38	☐ 97 Judges 20-21
☐ 46 Exodus 39-40	☐ 98 Ruth
☐ 47 Leviticus 1:1-5:13	☑ 99 1 Samuel 1-3
☐ 48 Leviticus 5:14-7:38	☑ 100 1 Samuel 4-7
☐ 49 Leviticus 8-10	☑ 101 1 Samuel 8-10
☐ 50 Leviticus 11-12	☐ 102 1 Samuel 11-13
☐ 51 Leviticus 13-14	☐ 103 1 Samuel 14-15
☐ 52 Leviticus 15-17	☐ 104 1 Samuel 16-17

Bible reading schedule
Day 105 - 199

- ☐ 105 1 Samuel 18-19; Psalm 59
- ☐ 106 1 Samuel 20-21; Psalm 56; 34
- ☐ 107 1 Samuel 22-23; 1 Chronicles 12:8-18; Psalm 52; 54; 63; 142
- ☐ 108 1 Samuel 24; Psalm 57; 1 Samuel 25
- ☐ 109 1 Samuel 26-29; 1 Chronicles 12:1-7, 19-22
- ☐ 110 1 Samuel 30-31; 1 Chronicles 10; 2 Samuel 1
- ☐ 111 2 Samuel 2-4
- ☐ 112 2 Samuel 5:1-6:11; 1 Chronicles 11:1-9; 2:23-40; 13:1-14:17
- ☐ 113 2 Samuel 22; Psalm 18
- ☐ 114 1 Chronicles 15-16; 2 Samuel 6:12-23; Psalm 96
- ☐ 115 Psalm 105; 2 Samuel 7; 1 Chronicles 17
- ☐ 116 2 Samuel 8-10; 1 Chronicles 18-19; Psalm 60
- ☐ 117 2 Samuel 11-12; 1 Chronicles 20:1-3; Psalm 51
- ☐ 118 2 Samuel 13-14
- ☐ 119 2 Samuel 15-17
- ☐ 120 Psalm 3; 2 Samuel 18-19
- ☐ 121 2 Samuel 20-21; 23:8-23; 1 Chronicles 20:4-8; 11:10-25
- ☐ 122 2 Samuel 23:24-24:25;
- ☐ 123 1 Chronicles 11:26-47; 21:1-30, 1 Chronicles 22-24
- ☐ 124 Psalm 30; 1 Chronicles 25-26
- ☐ 125 1 Chronicles 27-29
- ☐ 126 Psalms 5-7; 10; 11; 13; 17
- ☐ 127 Psalms 23; 26; 28; 31; 35
- ☐ 128 Psalms 41; 43; 46; 55; 61; 62; 64
- ☑ 129 Psalms 69-71; 77
- ☐ 130 Psalms 83; 86; 88; 91; 95
- ☐ 131 Psalms 108-9; 120-21; 140; 143-44
- ☐ 132 Psalms 1; 14-15; 36-37; 39
- ☐ 133 Psalms 40; 49-50; 73
- ☐ 134 Psalms 76; 82; 84; 90; 92; 112; 115
- ☐ 135 Psalms 8-9; 16; 19; 21; 24; 29
- ☐ 136 Psalms 33; 65-68
- ☐ 137 Psalms 75; 93-94; 97-100
- ☐ 138 Psalms 103-4; 113-14; 117
- ☐ 139 Psalm 119:1-88
- ☐ 140 Psalm 119:89-176
- ☐ 141 Psalms 122; 124; 133-36
- ☐ 142 Psalms 138-39; 145; 148; 150
- ☐ 143 Psalms 4; 12; 20; 25; 32; 38
- ☐ 144 Psalms 42; 53; 58; 81; 101; 111; 130-31; 141; 146
- ☐ 145 Psalms 2; 22; 27
- ☐ 146 Psalms 45; 47-48; 87; 110
- ☐ 147 1 Kings 1:1-2:12; 2 Samuel 23:1-7
- ☐ 148 1 Kings 2:13-3:28; 2 Chronicles 1:1-13
- ☐ 149 1 Kings 5-6; 2 Chronicles 2-3
- ☐ 150 1 Kings 7; 2 Chronicles 4
- ☐ 151 1 Kings 8; 2 Chronicles 5:1-7:10
- ☐ 152 1 Kings 9:1-10:13; 2 Chronicles 7:11-9:12
- ☐ 153 1 Kings 4; 10:14-29; 2 Chronicles 1:14-17; 9:13-28; Psalm 72
- ☐ 154 Proverbs 1-3
- ☐ 155 Proverbs 4-6
- ☐ 156 Proverbs 7-9
- ☐ 157 Proverbs 10-12
- ☐ 158 Proverbs 13-15
- ☐ 159 Proverbs 16-18
- ☐ 160 Proverbs 19-21
- ☐ 161 Proverbs 22-24
- ☐ 162 Proverbs 25-27
- ☐ 163 Proverbs 28-29
- ☐ 164 Proverbs 30-31; Psalm 127
- ☐ 165 Song of Solomon
- ☐ 166 1 Kings 11:1-40; Ecclesiastes 1-2
- ☐ 167 Ecclesiastes 3-7
- ☐ 168 Ecclesiastes 8-12; 1 Kings 11:41-43; 2 Chronicles 9:29-31
- ☐ 169 1 Kings 12; 2 Chronicles 10:1-11:17
- ☐ 170 1 Kings 13-14; 2 Chronicles 11:18-12:16
- ☐ 171 1 Kings 15:1-24; 2 Chronicles 13-16
- ☐ 172 1 Kings 15:25-16:34; 2 Chronicles 17; 1 Kings 17
- ☐ 173 1 Kings 18-19
- ☐ 174 1 Kings 20-21
- ☐ 175 1 Kings 22:1-40; 2 Chronicles 18
- ☐ 176 1 Kings 22:41-53; 2 Kings 1; 2 Chronicles 19:1-21:3
- ☐ 177 2 Kings 2-4
- ☐ 178 2 Kings 5-7
- ☐ 179 2 Kings 8-9; 2 Chronicles 21:4-22:9
- ☐ 180 2 Kings 10-11; 2 Chronicles 22:10-23:21
- ☐ 181 Joel
- ☐ 182 2 Kings 12-13; 2 Chronicles 24
- ☐ 183 2 Kings 14; 2 Chronicles 25; Jonah
- ☐ 184 Hosea 1-7
- ☐ 185 Hosea 8-14
- ☐ 186 2 Kings 15:1-7; 2 Chronicles 26; Amos 1-4
- ☐ 187 Amos 5-9; 2 Kings 15:8-18
- ☐ 188 Isaiah 1-4
- ☐ 189 2 Kings 15:19-38; 2 Chronicles 27; Isaiah 5-6
- ☐ 190 Micah
- ☐ 191 2 Kings 16; 2 Chronicles 28; Isaiah 7-8
- ☐ 192 Isaiah 9-12
- ☐ 193 Isaiah 13-16
- ☐ 194 Isaiah 17-22
- ☐ 195 Isaiah 23-27
- ☐ 196 Isaiah 28-30
- ☐ 197 Isaiah 31-35
- ☐ 198 2 Kings 18:1-8; 2 Chronicles 29-31
- ☐ 199 2 Kings 17; 18:9-37; 2 Chronicles 32:1-19; Isaiah 36

Bible reading schedule
Day 200 - 288

- [ ] 200 2 Kings 19; 2 Chronicles 32:20-23; Isaiah 37
- [ ] 201 2 Kings 20; 2 Chronicles 32:24-33; Isaiah 38-39
- [ ] 202 2 Kings 21:1-18; 2 Chronicles 33:1-20; Isaiah 40
- [ ] 203 Isaiah 41-43
- [ ] 204 Isaiah 44-47
- [ ] 205 Isaiah 48-51
- [ ] 206 Isaiah 52-57
- [ ] 207 Isaiah 58-62
- [ ] 208 Isaiah 63-66
- [ ] 209 2 Kings 21:19-26; 2 Chronicles 33:21-34:7; Zephaniah
- [ ] 210 Jeremiah 1-3
- [ ] 211 Jeremiah 4-6
- [ ] 212 Jeremiah 7-9
- [ ] 213 Jeremiah 10-13
- [ ] 214 Jeremiah 14-16
- [ ] 215 Jeremiah 17-20
- [ ] 216 2 Kings 22:1-23:28; 2 Chronicles 34:8-35:19
- [ ] 217 Nahum; 2 Kings 23:29-37; 2 Chronicles 35:20-36:5; Jeremiah 22:10-17
- [ ] 218 Jeremiah 26; Habakkuk
- [ ] 219 Jeremiah 46-47; 2 Kings 24:1-4, 7; 2 Chronicles 36:6-7; Jeremiah 25, 35
- [ ] 220 Jeremiah 36, 45, 48
- [ ] 221 Jeremiah 49:1-33; Daniel 1-2
- [ ] 222 Jeremiah 22:18-30; 2 Kings 24:5-20; 2 Chronicles 36:8-12; Jeremiah 37:1-2; 52:1-3; 24; 29
- [ ] 223 Jeremiah 27-28, 23
- [ ] 224 Jeremiah 50-51
- [ ] 225 Jeremiah 49:34-39; 34:1-22; Ezekiel 1-3
- [ ] 226 Ezekiel 4-7
- [ ] 227 Ezekiel 8-11
- [ ] 228 Ezekiel 12-14
- [ ] 229 Ezekiel 15-17
- [ ] 230 Ezekiel 18-20
- [ ] 231 Ezekiel 21-23
- [ ] 232 2 Kings 25:1; 2 Chronicles 36:13-16; Jeremiah 39:1; 52:4; Ezekiel 24; Jeremiah 21:1-22:9; 32:1-44
- [ ] 233 Jeremiah 30-31, 33
- [ ] 234 Ezekiel 25; 29:1-16; 30; 31
- [ ] 235 Ezekiel 26-28
- [ ] 236 Jeremiah 37:3-39:10; 52:5-30; 2 Kings 25:2-21; 2 Chronicles 36:17-21
- [ ] 237 2 Kings 25:22; Jeremiah 39:11-40:6; Lamentations 1-3
- [ ] 238 Lamentations 4-5; Obadiah
- [ ] 239 Jeremiah 40:7-44:30; 2 Kings 25:23-26
- [ ] 240 Ezekiel 33:21-36:38
- [ ] 241 Ezekiel 37-39
- [ ] 242 Ezekiel 32:1-33:20; Daniel 3
- [ ] 243 Ezekiel 40-42
- [ ] 244 Ezekiel 43-45
- [ ] 245 Ezekiel 46-48
- [ ] 246 Ezekiel 29:17-21; Daniel 4; Jeremiah 52:31-34; 2 Kings 25:27-30; Psalm 44
- [ ] 247 Psalms 74; 79-80; 89
- [ ] 248 Psalms 85; 102; 106; 123; 137
- [ ] 249 Daniel 7-8; 5
- [ ] 250 Daniel 9; 6
- [ ] 251 2 Chronicles 36:22-23; Ezra 1:1-4:5
- [ ] 252 Daniel 10-12
- [ ] 253 Ezra 4:6-6:13; Haggai
- [ ] 254 Zechariah 1-6
- [ ] 255 Zechariah 7-8; Ezra 6:14-22; Psalm 78
- [ ] 256 Psalms 107; 116; 118
- [ ] 257 Psalms 125-26; 128-29; 132; 147; 149
- [ ] 258 Zechariah 9-14
- [x] 259 Esther 1-4
- [ ] 260 Esther 5-10
- [ ] 261 Ezra 7-8
- [ ] 262 Ezra 9-10
- [ ] 263 Nehemiah 1-5
- [ ] 264 Nehemiah 6-7
- [ ] 265 Nehemiah 8-10
- [ ] 266 Nehemiah 11-13
- [ ] 267 Malachi
- [ ] 268 1 Chronicles 1-2
- [ ] 269 1 Chronicles 3-5
- [ ] 270 1 Chronicles 6
- [ ] 271 1 Chronicles 7:1-8:27
- [ ] 272 1 Chronicles 8:28-9:44
- [ ] 273 John 1:1-18; Mark 1:1; Luke 1:1-4; 3:23-38; Matthew 1:1-17
- [ ] 274 Luke 1:5-80
- [ ] 275 Matthew 1:18-2:23; Luke 2
- [ ] 276 Matthew 3:1-4:11; Mark 1:2-13; Luke 3:1-23; 4:1-13; John 1:19-34
- [ ] 277 John 1:35-3:36
- [ ] 278 John 4; Matthew 4:12-17; Mark 1:14-15; Luke 4:14-30
- [ ] 279 Mark 1:16-45; Matthew 4:18-25; 8:2-4, 14-17; Luke 4:31-5:16
- [ ] 280 Matthew 9:1-17; Mark 2:1-22; Luke 5:17-39
- [ ] 281 John 5; Matthew 12:1-21; Mark 2:23-3:12; Luke 6:1-11
- [ ] 282 Matthew 5; Mark 3:13-19; Luke 6:12-36
- [ ] 283 Matthew 6-7; Luke 6:37-49
- [ ] 284 Luke 7; Matthew 8:1, 5-13; 11:2-30
- [ ] 285 Matthew 12:22-50; Mark 3:20-35; Luke 8:1-21
- [ ] 286 Mark 4:1-34; Matthew 13:1-53
- [ ] 287 Mark 4:35-5:43; Matthew 8:18, 23-34; 9:18-34; Luke 8:22-56
- [ ] 288 Mark 6:1-30; Matthew 13:54-58; 9:35-11:1; 14:1-12; Luke 9:1-10

Bible reading schedule
Day 289 - 365

- ☐ 289 Matthew 14:13-36; Mark 6:31-56; Luke 9:11-17; John 6:1-21
- ☐ 290 John 6:22-7:1; Matthew 15:1-20; Mark 7:1-23
- ☐ 291 Matthew 15:21-16:20; Mark 7:24-8:30; Luke 9:18-21
- ☐ 292 Matthew 16:21-17:27; Mark 8:31-9:32; Luke 9:22-45
- ☐ 293 Matthew 18; 8:19-22; Mark 9:33-50; Luke 9:46-62; John 7:2-10
- ☐ 294 John 7:11-8:59
- ☐ 295 Luke 10:1-11:36
- ☐ 296 Luke 11:37-13:21
- ☐ 297 John 9-10
- ☐ 298 Luke 13:22-15:32
- ☐ 299 Luke 16:1-17:10; John 11:1-54
- ☐ 300 Luke 17:11-18:17; Matthew 19:1-15; Mark 10:1-16
- ☐ 301 Matthew 19:16-20:28; Mark 10:17-45; Luke 18:18-34
- ☐ 302 Matthew 20:29-34; 26:6-13; Mark 10:46-52; 14:3-9; Luke 18:35-19:28; John 11:55-12:11
- ☐ 303 Matthew 21:1-22; Mark 11:1-26; Luke 19:29-48; John 12:12-50
- ☐ 304 Matthew 21:23-22:14; Mark 11:27-12:12; Luke 20:1-19
- ☐ 305 Matthew 22:15-46; Mark 12:13-37; Luke 20:20-44
- ☐ 306 Matthew 23; Mark 12:38-44; Luke 20:45-21:4
- ☐ 307 Matthew 24:1-31; Mark 13:1-27; Luke 21:5-27
- ☐ 308 Matthew 24:32-26:5, 14-16; Mark 13:28-14:2, 10-11; Luke 21:28-22:6
- ☐ 309 Matthew 26:17-29; Mark 14:12-25; Luke 22:7-38; John 13
- ☐ 310 John 14-16
- ☐ 311 John 17:1-18:1; Matthew 26:30-46; Mark 14:26-42; Luke 22:39-46
- ☐ 312 Matthew 26:47-75; Mark 14:43-72; Luke 22:47-65; John 18:2-27
- ☐ 313 Matthew 27:1-26; Mark 15:1-15; Luke 22:66-23:25; John 18:28-19:16
- ☐ 314 Matthew 27:27-56; Mark 15:16-41; Luke 23:26-49; John 19:17-30
- ☐ 315 Matthew 27:57-28:8; Mark 15:42-16:8; Luke 23:50-24:12; John 19:31-20:10
- ☐ 316 Matthew 28:9-20; Mark 16:9-20; Luke 24:13-53; John 20:11-21:25
- ☐ 317 Acts 1-2
- ☐ 318 Acts 3-5
- ☐ 319 Acts 6:1-8:1
- ☐ 320 Acts 8:2-9:43
- ☐ 321 Acts 10-11
- ☐ 322 Acts 12-13
- ☐ 323 Acts 14-15
- ☐ 324 Galatians 1-3
- ☐ 325 Galatians 4-6
- ☑ 326 James
- ☐ 327 Acts 16:1-18:11
- ☐ 328 1 Thessalonians
- ☐ 329 2 Thessalonians; Acts 18:12-19:22
- ☐ 330 1 Corinthians 1-4
- ☐ 331 1 Corinthians 5-8
- ☐ 332 1 Corinthians 9-11
- ☐ 333 1 Corinthians 12-14
- ☐ 334 1 Corinthians 15-16
- ☐ 335 Acts 19:23-20:1; 2 Corinthians 1-4
- ☐ 336 2 Corinthians 5-9
- ☐ 337 2 Corinthians 10-13
- ☐ 338 Romans 1-3
- ☐ 339 Romans 4-6
- ☐ 340 Romans 7-8
- ☐ 341 Romans 9-11
- ☐ 342 Romans 12-15
- ☐ 343 Romans 16; Acts 20:2-21:16
- ☐ 344 Acts 21:17-23:35
- ☐ 345 Acts 24-26
- ☐ 346 Acts 27-28
- ☐ 347 Ephesians 1-3
- ☐ 348 Ephesians 4-6
- ☐ 349 Colossians
- ☐ 350 Philippians
- ☐ 351 Philemon; 1 Timothy 1-3
- ☐ 352 1 Timothy 4-6; Titus
- ☐ 353 2 Timothy
- ☐ 354 1 Peter
- ☐ 355 Jude; 2 Peter
- ☐ 356 Hebrews 1:1-5:10
- ☐ 357 Hebrews 5:11-9:28
- ☐ 358 Hebrews 10-11
- ☐ 359 Hebrews 12-13; 2 John; 3 John
- ☐ 360 1 John
- ☐ 361 Revelation 1-3
- ☐ 362 Revelation 4-9
- ☐ 363 Revelation 10-14
- ☐ 364 Revelation 15-18
- ☐ 365 Revelation 19-22

From the Liberty Bible, King James Version. Copyright ©1975, Thomas Nelson, Inc. Publishers. Used by permission.

Aren't you glad God is gracious and kind to us, even when we don't deserve it? This week you'll see how God continued to love and be gracious to Israel in spite of the nation's history of rebellion and ingratitude.

Week 1

prayer focus for this week

Keep a positive attitude

the**Question** the**Answer**

What is the writer saying?

How Can I apply this to my life?

sunday • Psalm 77:1-20

Q

A

DIGGING DEEPER • Have you ever thought God was out to get you? Have you ever had a feeling that He had something against you? Some would nod their heads and say we've been there. We've accused God. Blamed Him. Told Him we weren't getting a fair deal. Prayed. Cried. But like the Psalmist, we only did this for a little while. Then we realized how wonderful He truly is. We need to remember how He saved us, forgave us of our sins, and gave us a brand new start. And as we realize this, then our frustration gradually turns into praise. We then realize that God really does love us and He's not out to get us. **What do you do with your frustrations? Have they ever caused you to praise God? Have you ever let them?**

monday • Psalm 78:1-10

DIGGING DEEPER • What kind of legacy do you want to leave your children? It may be a little early to be thinking about that, but do it anyway. Is it important to you that they know you were a star on the basketball team or a member of the cheerleading squad? Certainly accomplishments have their place, but the next generation of your family needs to be aware of the relationship you had with the living God. If we really believe that Jesus is the only hope for this world, then we'll be careful to make certain that Christianity doesn't die with our generation. Pass it on to your children. Tell stories to your grandchildren. Don't let the faith that was passed on to you stop with your generation.
What steps can you begin taking now to leave a legacy of faith for your children? Maybe you could write out your testimony.

tuesday • Psalm 78:17-31

DIGGING DEEPER • Quit complaining! Have you ever wanted to say this to someone? Maybe you were at school or perhaps you were on a short-term mission trip. Whatever the case, someone begins to complain. Rather than be thankful for all God has done in their life up to that point or the results that have taken place on the mission trip, this person complains – about food, facilities, weather, whatever. We all probably have been guilty of complaining at times, but we need to make an effort to stay positive. Let's remember Jesus paid a debt too great for us to pay. He rose from the dead. He's preparing a place for us in Heaven even today, and He is coming soon to take us home with Him.
Do you need to stop complaining? What can you thank God for today, despite your problems and circumstances?

wednesday • Psalm 78:32-44

Q
A

DIGGING DEEPER • Have you forgotten about all that God has done for you? Do you need someone to remind you? Let me refresh your memory. If you are a Christian, the Bible says the Lord saved you, called you, set you apart, wrote your name down in Heaven, and gave you His Spirit to comfort, encourage, and live within you. And these are just some of His benefits. Yet, how often do we think about these great truths? We don't, and that's a problem. Christians today are just like Israel of old. We *forget* a lot, and as a result of our forgetting, our lives end up in shambles. While Israel remembered a little about God, they forgot a lot. What about you?
What do you tend to forget about our God? What can you do to remember what God has done for you?

thursday • Psalm 78:45-55

Q
A

DIGGING DEEPER • Have you ever tested your parents' patience? You know, like complaining over what food they give you to eat, the place you live, the nice clothes you wear, and the care they provide? Have you responded to their love and kindness with a bad attitude? It's not what they deserve. Israel did the same thing to God. God did so many wonderful works for Israel. He rescued them from slavery in Egypt, led them through the wilderness, showed His power through many miracles, and eliminated their enemies just to name a few. And their response to God was basically, *So what? Who cares?* In short, they rebelled just like some of us do as teenagers. Don't let this happen to you.
Are you thankful for your parents and all they've done for you? How about God and all He's done? What could you do to show thanks?

friday • Psalm 78:59-72

DIGGING DEEPER • Sin has its consequences. Ask Israel. As Israel continually rebelled against Jehovah God, they were surprised to see He still dealt with them in love; however, there were still consequences. He allowed the ark of God to be stolen by Israel's enemies. He let Israel's enemies come in and kill many of His chosen people. He would not tolerate their sin; and while some might argue that we have a kinder, gentler God today, He tolerates sin no more than He did in Old Testament times. For this reason, if no other, it is of vital importance that we daily confess sin and repent of it as well. We cannot tolerate sin in our lives as the children of Israel did.
Do you need to be honest and confess a sin to God right now? Do you need to get right with someone else?

saturday • Psalm 79:1-17

DIGGING DEEPER • Does it ever seem to you that God is slow to mete out justice or that He is unfair? Why is it that the wicked can get away with murder and experience no consequences, while the righteous are punished despite their clean hearts and hands? Why doesn't God do something about it? Asaph, most likely the writer of this Psalm, relates to how we often feel. It's easy to become frustrated as we live the Christian life, but be assured: God is consistent. Asaph knew this. The next time you feel overwhelmed by circumstances out of your control, be reminded that God loves you and He's not out to get you.
What frustrates you about the world around you? How might you respond to someone who says God is inconsistent?

37

Have you ever prayed and felt like God was deaf to your prayers? If so, you're not alone. In fact, this week, you'll read several prayers from individuals who accused God of not listening or responding to them.

Week 2

prayer focus for this week

What is the writer saying?

How can I apply this to my life?

sunday • Psalm 80:1-19

Q
A

DIGGING DEEPER • Thankfully, our God gives second chances, and third ones, too. With this in mind, Asaph prays for a second chance. In Israel's case, God had given them many chances before. He gave them second chances with Moses as their leader. Joshua saw God give second chances. The Book of Judges shows God giving chance after chance after chance. God gave second chances throughout Scripture to men such as David, Jonah, and Peter among others. And so Asaph, on behalf of Israel, says, *God, give us another chance.* And while we don't have a recorded response, Scripture tells us God answered, and continues to give second chances today.

Have you ever asked God for a second chance at something? How did you do with that second chance?

monday • Psalm 81:1-16

Q
A

DIGGIHG DEEPER · Do you like to sing? Most people do. So when Scripture says, "Sing" or "Make a joyful noise," we should have no problem obeying God. But let's be clear about one thing: We should love to sing to God more than to anyone else! While we can enjoy various styles and types of music, if we're going to sing, nothing compares to singing to and about God. I Love You Lord, Lord, I Lift Your Name on High, and other songs that have God at their center are favorites of many, not just because they have God as their subject, but because their message is straight out of Scripture. If you're going to sing, sing to God. He gave you your voice and He asks for you to sing to Him. What are you waiting for?

What's your favorite song about God? Why? Could singing be a part of your devotions?

tuesday • Psalm 82:1-8

Q
A

DIGGIHG DEEPER · Have you ever stood before a judge? Regardless, you've more than likely turned your television on to see Judge Judy staring back at you. Judge Judy is a real judge who presides over real court cases. She has the ability to humiliate and intimidate almost everyone who stands before her. It doesn't matter who you are, when you're in her courtroom, there's no doubt who's in charge. She is! However, as intimidating as she might be, she pales in comparison to the One we will all stand before one day, God Himself. He is our Judge and we should live our lives with the realization that one day we will enter His courtroom and give an account of how we lived our lives.

Are you ready to stand before God in His courtroom? If not, what steps can you take to get ready?

wednesday • Psalm 83:1-18

DIGGING DEEPER • Don't mess with Israel. This can be said because it is indicated in Scripture. In fact, Scripture is clear that anyone who opposes Israel opposes God. Historically, Israel has had many enemies. From the Egyptians, to the Philistines and Babylonians, even to the Palestinians today, Israel has faced her share of foes. While many have come and gone, Israel remains. Is this a coincidence? No. Providence? Absolutely. God has protected Israel throughout the years, despite any outward appearances that would indicate otherwise. He will continue to protect Israel in the days to come. **Why would anyone oppose God? Are you opposing God by the way you live?**

thursday • Psalm 84:1-12

DIGGING DEEPER • Would you rather have the nicest home imaginable on earth or be the person who holds the doors in God's house? I know many who would choose the first of these two options, but what about you? We all know the spiritual answer. As Christians, we should never choose the option that leaves God out of the equation. But in reality, many of us make that choice every day. It's time we stand with the Psalmist and echo his words of wisdom. There really is no comparison between God's dwelling place and the homes of people. Even though God's dwelling place is fabulous, God's presence is the most important of all. **What do you imagine Heaven will be like? Is your mental picture comparable to any place you've been to on earth?**

friday • Psalm 85:1-13

DIGGING DEEPER • God keeps His promises. Hold on, perhaps you just skimmed that first sentence. Read it again, and this time, really think as you read it. Now, do you agree with this sentence? Be honest. Whatever your opinion of this initial statement, it is true. It would not be right for us to say anything contrary to this. We sing songs about His promises and in fact, our very salvation depends on God's promise. As you look at this Psalm, it starts with praise over the results of past promises and ends with promises for the future with many interpreting it as the coming of the Messiah, Jesus Christ. While you and I may break promises from time to time, God never has and never will. You can count on Him!
How has God kept His promises in your own life? Has He been faithful and loving?

saturday • Psalm 86:1-17

DIGGING DEEPER • Prayer works. You've probably seen it work in your own life as well in the lives of others. But some people often view prayer in a negative light. There are those who even consider prayer as selfish. While we may agree that our prayer life should not be completely self-centered, we can't help but notice how David, *a man after God's own heart*, prays for himself. He prays to be heard, protected, blessed, and forgiven among other requests for himself. Sure, he gives thanks to God and praises his Father, but the majority of his prayer involves what he'd like to see God do in his own life. Is this a selfish prayer? No, and it wouldn't hurt the cause of Christ for more of us to be more open and direct with God and pray similar prayers to our Father.
What part of this prayer sticks out to you? Do you need to pray something similar?

God always keeps His promises. You can count on Him in whatever situation you may find yourself. This week you'll read about a promise He made to King David thousands of years ago and how He kept that promise just like He said He would despite the doubts of some.

prayer focus for this week

the Question
the Answer

What is the writer saying?

How Can I apply this to my life?

sunday • Psalm 87:1-7

Q
A

DIGGING DEEPER • God loves Israel. He always has and always will. He had Israel in mind when He moved Abraham from the comfort of his home; when Joseph was in prison in the land of Egypt; when Moses grew up in Pharaoh's house; when King David slew Goliath; and when He sent His Son Jesus to earth. He still has Israel in mind today when the nation's very existence is being threatened by terrorists. He still loves Israel and chooses to have His name exalted by them and desires that they love Him in return. As believers, we should desire to exalt His name as well.

Why do you think God loves Israel so much? Why does He love you so much? Does God's love for you and Israel depend on what you do or how great God is?

monday • Psalm 88:1-18

DIGGING DEEPER • Have you ever felt like God wasn't listening to your prayers? How did you respond? Did you try yelling at the top of your lungs? How about writing out a prayer? That's what some imagine the writer of this Psalm did. After begging and pleading with God for many years to be healed from some kind of sickness, the author takes his pen and begins to write what he has been praying for so many years. Not a bad idea. In fact, it's an excellent idea and it would do us all good to take some time and write out a prayer to God about our concerns, desires, and heartaches. Even in difficult times, we should still find things for which we can rejoice.
Have you ever tried writing out your prayers? How might this help your prayer life?

tuesday • Psalm 89:1-18

DIGGING DEEPER • We serve a faithful God. He's faithful in little things and in big things. He's consistent, reliable, and trustworthy. You can count on Him. While everyone around you fails or disappoints you, He continues to be faithful. In spite of our own times of unfaithfulness, His faithfulness abounds still. Every second of every minute… of every hour… of every day… of every year, God remains faithful. He is faithful in His love. He is faithful in His mercy. And thankfully, He is faithful in His forgiveness of our sins. As we examine our lives we see He's been faithful to us. You'll find He's been just as faithful to you too.
How has God been faithful to you? How have you shown Him your faithfulness?

wednesday • Psalm 89:19-37

DIGGING DEEPER • Have you ever made a covenant with someone? I'm talking about a serious agreement, not some passing promise. You made a pact with a person and together agreed on the details. God did this with King David. God's promise with David has come to be known as the Davidic Covenant. In short, the Davidic Covenant can be described as God's promise to David that the line of kings would go through his family, regardless of the actions of future kings. God assures David of this and gives him His word that He will never break this covenant. As you probably already know, God never broke that promise. In fact, Jesus Himself, the King of kings, was a descendant of David. What a covenant! What a God!
What covenant has God made with you? Can you count on Him?

thursday • Psalm 89:38-52

DIGGING DEEPER • Do you play the *blame game*? In other words, do you blame others before you ever take the time to see if you had any responsibility in the situation? Let's admit it. We've blamed others prematurely. We've pointed the finger at others when we should have taken a closer look at ourselves. Israel sure did. Instead of confessing sin and asking for forgiveness, Israel blamed God. The Psalmist, speaking on behalf of the nation, doesn't like what he sees happening in Israel. And rather than point the finger at his own nation, he chooses to blame God. Unfortunately we do the same thing. We bring things upon ourselves and then blame God. It wasn't right for Israel to blame God for their sin and it is not right for us to do so either.
Why do we blame God? Should we ever blame God?

friday · Psalm 90:1-17

DIGGING DEEPER · Did you know that Moses wrote several of the Psalms? You do now. In this particular Psalm, he begins by telling God what an awesome God He is. He continues by confessing his and Israel's sins to God. He wraps up his words with a series of petitions. Not a bad way to pray. In fact, this could be easily used as a model for prayer. Begin with worship, continue with confession, and close by letting your personal requests be made known to God. Why not follow Moses's pattern of prayer today? Change it a little bit, but say some similar things to God when you talk to Him today.
Is worship a regular part of your prayer life? How about confession? How about personal requests?

saturday · Psalm 91:1-16

DIGGING DEEPER · Have you ever been scared? Really afraid? As a child, no doubt, there were instances when you were fearful. In those times, the very reading of Scripture can calm our fears. It would tell us about a God Whom we could trust to look out for us and take care of us. We should teach our own children these same truths. One of the best passages to start with is Psalm 91. We see a picture of God as our refuge, shelter, and place of safety in this Psalm. We're encouraged to not let darkness, sickness, and evil alarm us, but to trust in our God.
When you are worried or scared, do you remember that God is your refuge and He will take care of you? How can you remind yourself that God is your refuge?

What is God like? Have you ever wondered that? Wonder no more, as this week we'll get a glimpse of God by reading about a number of His characteristics including His love, faithfulness, and sovereignty.

prayer focus for this week

the Question
the Answer

What is the writer saying?

How Can I apply this to my life?

sunday • Psalm 92:1-15

Q

A

DIGGING DEEPER • It is a good thing to give thanks. We appreciate it when people say thank you. God also appreciates it and values our expressions of thanks. If you're not in the habit of giving God thanks, then start today with the fact that He is the Rock who is unfailing, loving, faithful, fruitful, and upright. We're not talking about just thanking Him for meals. We're speaking of a much broader type of thanksgiving. Thanks for life and breath. Thanks for specific blessings, both physical and spiritual. Family, friends, creation, and salvation are all things for which we should thank God. It really is a good thing to give thanks to the Lord. Christians should do it a lot more often.
What can you give thanks to God for today? When was the last time you told Him *thank You*?

monday • Psalm 93:1-5

DIGGING DEEPER · God is King. There's no doubt about who rules and reigns in this universe. It is God and God alone. He has been the King since eternity past and will continue to be King forever. The earth and seas recognize the fact that He is King, and all creation agrees as well. As you look closely at this Psalm, you'll notice several characteristics about this King: He is majestic, omnipotent, immovable, eternal, mighty, and holy. In a phrase, He is the *King of kings*. And because He is King, we owe Him the respect and reverence any other king deserves and much more.
How does one act before royalty? How can this apply to our relationship with God? How can you honor your King today?

tuesday • Psalm 94:1-11

DIGGING DEEPER · Have you ever questioned authority? Sure you have! At some point in your life you've questioned your parents, teachers, and even pastors. In fact, most of you have probably even questioned the ultimate authority, God Himself. Maybe you've wondered why He allowed a loving and godly grandparent to die, or perhaps you've questioned why a friend was diagnosed with cancer. To a certain extent, we've all questioned God. We've all had those feelings that He wasn't paying attention to us and our problems. The fact of the matter is that God is aware of our problems. He understands our situation, and His timing is perfect. You can count on Him.
What have you questioned God about in the past? Do you still have some questions?

wednesday • Psalm 94:12-23

DIGGING DEEPER • We're safe with God. He's our fortress, our rock, and our hiding place. When evil and all its fury begin to come after us, we have a shelter in our God. When godless people do all they can to destroy and attack our faith, our God is there for us. When we're in danger of allowing a sin to become a habit in our lives, our God will protect us. We obviously must do our part to run to our God and let Him be our Rock. When we do, there is no doubt that we will understand that this psalm is true: God is our Rock!
When has God been your Rock? What do other people you know lean on when troubles come?

thursday • Psalm 95:1-11

DIGGING DEEPER • How are we supposed to approach God in our worship? Should we be *at attention* as a Marine recruit might find himself at basic training? Is it necessary to bow our heads, fold our hands, and close our eyes? The Psalmist's purpose here is not to give us a complete list of ways to approach God in worship, but he does offer several suggestions. First, according to Jewish tradition, it is acceptable to prostrate oneself (lay flat on the ground face down). Bowing and kneeling are also appropriate. Certainly there are other methods as well. The point, however, is that you worship. Whatever your method or style may be in approaching God, do it with a pure heart and clean hands.
How do you approach God in worship or prayer? How do you think God responds to your particular approach?

friday • Psalm 96:1-13

Q

A

DIGGING DEEPER • Wouldn't you like to see our nation come to know Christ? What about the whole world? Sure, it seems out of reach, but it didn't prevent David from pleading for it. His desire should be our desire today. Just as he pleaded with the earth to recognize who God is, to give Him the praise He deserves, and to worship and respect Him, we should make a similar plea to the citizens of our cities, states, country, and world. Will we be heard? By some, yes; by all, probably not. Should we make an effort anyway? Absolutely! It's time to celebrate the Coming One.
How do you think the average American views God? How do you view Him? What is one way you can impact the world for Christ?

saturday • Psalm 97:1-12

DIGGING DEEPER • Do you hate evil? If you're a Christian, you're supposed to. In fact, your love for God should be evident in your hatred of evil. If you really love God you'll hate particular sins, the results of sin, sin in your own life, and sin in the lives of those you love. You'll cringe at the thought of sin, daily confess your own sin, and urge others to avoid sin in general. Sin will annoy you, bother you, and even sicken you to an extent. So I ask you again, do you hate evil? We are to hate evil by being committed to a life that reflects faithful obedience to God's righteous standards. If you're a Christian, you're supposed to. Enough said.
How do you think God feels about sin? How do you feel when you sin? Does it bother you? What should you do with your sin?

What does it mean to praise and worship God? You'll soon find out, as you'll be faced this week with Psalm after Psalm written to God for one purpose: praise and worship.

Week 5

prayer focus for this week

the Question the Answer

What is the writer saying?

How can I apply this to my life?

sunday • Psalm 98:1-9

Q

A

DIGGING DEEPER • We sing about Jesus at Christmas time... *Joy to the world, the Lord is come*. Yes, He came as the Savior, but He's coming again as the Messiah. As such, He is coming to rule and reign on the earth. Psalm 98 is what is known as a Messianic Psalm. Simply stated, it is a Psalm about the Messiah. Specifically, the Psalmist shares with us several truths about the Messiah. First, the Messiah is the victorious deliverer of His people. Second, the Messiah is the King of kings who is more than worthy of our praise. Third, He is the judge of all people. We can anticipate the day when Christ returns as the Messiah, the Deliverer, the King, and the Judge.

Are you ready for the Messiah to return? Why or why not? What changes could you make in your life to be ready?

monday • Psalm 99:1-9

DIGGING DEEPER • God is holy. He is without sin. Perfect. Untouched by evil. God's attribute of holiness demands a response from us. First, we are to recognize God's holiness and offer Him the praise He justly deserves. Secondly, we should allow His holiness to affect us in such a way that others see Him and His holiness through us. As Christians, we have a responsibility to live holy, separated lives. Will we be sinless? No. Should we strive to be? Yes. We must all make a better effort to be holy, even as our God is holy. Even if we attempt to live holy lives and fail, there is still forgiveness and an opportunity to pick up and go on from where we left off.
What are some hindrances to holiness? What can we do about those hindrances?

tuesday • Psalm 100:1-5

DIGGING DEEPER • Is Thanksgiving the only time you tell God, *Thank You*? Honestly, do you regularly take time to let God know how thankful you are for all He has done for you? He certainly deserves our thanks and appreciation, doesn't He? Absolutely! So we should live our lives in a continual state of thankfulness to our God. We should thank Him for spiritual blessings such as eternal life, joy, and peace. We should thank Him for physical blessings like life, breath, food, and shelter. We should thank Him for relational blessings including family, friends, and loved ones. There's a lot to be thankful for. So let's get to it! Singing about His goodness is one way to show thankfulness.
How often do you tell God that you're thankful? When was the last time you told Him *thank you* for sending His Son Jesus to die for you?

51

wednesday • Psalm 101:1-8

Q
A

DIGGING DEEPER · In three short words, *live the life* summarizes what every Christian teenager needs to do. Psalm 101 is a mini-instructional manual on just how to live a victorious life. It involves our attitude and our actions. The Psalmist advises us through his own experiences to give God praise, live a blameless life, and refuse to look at anything impure. He explains how he seeks to avoid the company of evildoers and, at the same time, pursues the company of the godly. In general, this is great truth for the new believer or the Christian who's been there and done that. It's time for us to live the life and live it more abundantly!

How would you describe your Christian life? What would others say?

thursday • Psalm 102:1-14

Q
A

DIGGING DEEPER · Have you ever felt hopeless? You know, that overwhelming feeling that we sometimes experience as a result of life's various problems. The Psalmist describes this feeling of being overwhelmed very well. He describes being helpless before God and desiring for God to hear and answer him. He explains that there are physical side effects that accompany his hopelessness. On and on, the Psalmist describes the hopelessness that he feels as he lives his life. But, after his words of struggle are finished, he changes his tone and gives praise to his God. In the end, we must all learn to turn our problems over to our great God.

When major problems come, how do you feel? Pressured? Hopeless? Sick? How can God help you in those times?

friday • Psalm 102:15-28

DIGGIHG DEEPER • God never changes. He's always the same. The old hymn says, *Yesterday, today, forever, Jesus is the same.* And He is. The God of the Old Testament is the same God we serve today. Though times have changed, He hasn't. Though cultures are different, He isn't. While it seems that everything else has changed in one way or another over the years, God hasn't. He's forever constant, forever faithful, forever loving, and forever forgiving. He's not going anywhere, and we can count on Him even when things are really rough. That's seeing things from God's perspective… and it's always better than seeing it from man's perspective.

What are some changes that have taken place in your life recently? How can our *unchanging* God help you?

saturday • Psalm 103:1-22

DIGGIHG DEEPER • Have you ever taken the time to write down how God has blessed you? David did. He praised the Lord for a number of things in this Psalm. He generally thanked God for love and life. He specifically thanked God for being merciful and gracious. David focuses in this Psalm on giving God praise for forgiving him of his sins, even separating them as far as the east is from the west. For those of you attempting to figure out just how far away this is, put your calculators away. David is speaking in infinite terms. A key word might be everlasting. It is limitless. In fact, another way of putting it is to say that God forgives you completely and permanently.

Have you ever thanked God for forgiving you? What about lately? If there is still unconfessed sin, why not ask Him now for forgiveness?

Who are you most thankful for in your life? We all appreciate those who love and provide for us or do things on our behalf. Nevertheless, have you seriously considered all that God has done for you? Paul will teach us this week that we are truly loved and blessed by God through the Lord Jesus Christ.

Week 6

prayer focus for this week

the Question
the Answer

What is the writer saying?

How Can I apply this to my life?

sunday • Ephesians 1:1-6

Q
A

DIGGING DEEPER • Have you ever asked yourself, "Who am I?" That is a question we all ask at some point in our lives. At salvation, we become *in Christ* through the forgiveness of our sins, and we become *saints*, which means we are *set apart for God*. We must decide to live out our position (in Christ) every day with our actions. We may not always act like saints, but that is who we are *in Christ*. Meditate on these things. Paul points out what we as saints have. First, God chose us (v. 4). Second, He adopted us as His children (v. 5). Third, *we have all spiritual blessings …in Christ* (v. 3). Fourth, we can be holy and without blame before Him in love (v. 4).

Who are you? Are you a saint? Praise God for the four areas listed above. Make a list of what God has done for you lately.

monday • Ephesians 1:7-14

Q
A

DIGGING DEEPER • As you read a mystery have you ever gotten frustrated with the author for not revealing enough information? Early in this book (vv. 8-10) Paul tells us that, in God's grace, the believer has the resources necessary to comprehend God's will and purpose. The *inheritance* we have can be read two ways: *We have obtained an inheritance* (v. 11), or We were made His inheritance (Romans 8:17). Both are true. We are also *sealed with the Holy Spirit* (v. 14). This is a mark of ownership and a pledge from God that our redemption will be completed in Heaven.

Do you understand God's will for your life? Are you sealed with the Holy Spirit? Ask God and a leader to help you understand what you have in Christ.

tuesday • Ephesians 1:15-23

Q
A

DIGGING DEEPER • Have you ever watched a friend struggle with his need for salvation? You rejoice when he decides to accept the Lord. When you have the opportunity to lead someone to the Lord, the very first thing you do is pray for his spiritual growth. That is what Paul is doing here after spending nearly three years with the believers in Asia (Acts 18-21). He wants them to know how to grow in the Lord, by praying for God to give them wisdom, knowledge, and understanding (vv. 17-18). Also, he prays that they would realize the calling they have in Christ and the power He has over the past, present, and future.

Who have you led to the Lord lately? Pray for yourself and a friend to grow in wisdom, knowledge, and understanding of what you have in Jesus.

wednesday • Ephesians 2:1-7

Q
A

DIGGING DEEPER • Wow! What a difference Jesus makes in our lives! The first few verses tell what we were before coming to Christ (i.e. dead in sin, disobedient to God, following the world, an enemy of God, a child of wrath, and pursuing selfish desires). It was not a pretty picture. Paul tells us in the next several verses what God has done for us through His grace. We became spiritually alive and are elevated to a new level of life. Better still is that we can have a continuous relationship with Christ! When we contrast who we once were with who we now are in Christ, we can only marvel at God's great love, grace, and mercy, given freely to undeserving sinners like us. Believers have much for which to be thankful. **How has Christ changed your life? Make a list comparing how your life was before and after Christ came in. Take time to really thank Him!**

thursday • Ephesians 2:8-13

Q
A

DIGGING DEEPER • If you have been a Christian for any length of time, you've probably memorized verses 8 and 9. They even may have been instrumental in your coming to Christ and understanding the Gospel. Look again at the three main words. *Grace* is God giving us something we don't deserve. *Faith* allows us to accept God's grace. The *gift* comes from the hand of God. We can't boast in something we didn't earn, buy, work for, etc. When we understand all that the Lord has done for us, our response should be to do whatever He asks. His desire is for us to do good works, to do His will, and to do whatever He has planned for us. **Praise God for His grace and gift of salvation! In every choice you make today ask if it is something that will bring Him glory.**

friday • Ephesians 2:14-18

DIGGING DEEPER • There are many prejudices in our world, but praise God, He is not prejudiced! There was a huge division between Jews and Gentiles during the first century. Paul teaches that while they were once alienated, they are now one in Christ. Through Jesus, we are each reconciled first to God, and then we can be reconciled with others because we share Jesus in our hearts. His desire is for us to work as one to do His good work, to not be divided, and to reach those around us with the Gospel of the Lord Jesus Christ. The bottom line is this—whether Jew or Gentile, all believers have a common denominator—new life in Christ.

Do you have Jesus as a *common denominator* with other believers? Take time today to thank Jesus for removing the barrier.

saturday • Ephesians 2:19-22

DIGGING DEEPER • Have you ever watched a building go up? Time is spent on getting the foundation just right so the rest of the building will fit together perfectly. Paul is saying we are a picture of the work of Christ in our lives. We are a living temple built of people who are called *living stones* (1 Peter 2:4-8). Christ is the foundation and cornerstone. Every line in the building is justified only when it is aligned with Him. What a privilege it is to be the habitation of God! How important it is that our lives, individually and corporately, demonstrate that indwelling relationship.

Are you part of Christ's Temple with Jesus as the foundation? Welcome all believers to fellowship with you, especially those who are different from you.

Do you ever get tired of people telling you to just live for Jesus without really explaining how or why? This week Paul will reveal a mystery about Jews and Gentiles. He will offer practical advice on how and why we can live a successful Christian life in unity with others.

Week 7

prayer focus for this week

the Question
the Answer

What is the writer saying?

How Can I apply this to my life?

sunday • Ephesians 3:1-7

Q
A

DIGGING DEEPER • Why do you think Paul claimed himself to be *the prisoner of the Lord Jesus Christ* when he was in a Roman prison? It's because he knew Whom he served and the reason he was there. It didn't matter what the Romans did to him. He felt compelled by the Holy Spirit to explain the equality that Jews and Gentiles have in Jesus. Their unity in Christ was a *mystery* he was sent to reveal to both groups. This is the third time he addresses this issue (Ephesians 1:10-12; 2:14-18; 3:6-7), so it must be something important for us to understand and remember. We are *of the same body and partakers of His promise in Christ* (v. 6).
We should accept anyone into fellowship who claims the Lord Jesus Christ as his Lord and Savior. Be looking for someone to fellowship with today.

monday • Ephesians 3:8-13

DIGGING DEEPER • A thousand-piece puzzle takes a long time and requires great patience to put together. Part of the problem is that some of the pieces look alike, but don't fit where you think they should. The Old Testament writers had different pieces of the puzzle. Now Paul is humbled to be given the responsibility of putting the pieces together by proclaiming the (puzzle) *mystery* of the church to the world. Because of the grace of God, Jews and Gentiles are now one body in Christ. They are called the church, and through them the world is to learn of the glories of the Gospel.

Does your piece of the puzzle fit with those around you revealing the Gospel to others? Decide to share Jesus with someone today.

tuesday • Ephesians 3:14-21

DIGGING DEEPER • Have you ever been to Niagara Falls? Surely, you've seen pictures of this marvel of God's creation. Niagara Falls has just a fraction of the power that Paul is praying for *the whole family in heaven and earth*. Paul makes four requests for God's people. First, He asks they be strengthened by the Holy Spirit. Second, he asks that Christ would feel at home in their hearts. Third, he wants them to comprehend, know, and experience Christ's love. Fourth, He wants believers to understand the unlimited source from which we can draw for every need.

Pray for strength, for Christ to feel at home in your heart, to know how much Jesus loves you, and to understand the unlimited resources we have in the Holy Spirit. Write down one way you will live your life differently today.

wednesday • Ephesians 4:1-10

DIGGING DEEPER • At home or school, have you ever been told what to do, but not how or why? It's frustrating, isn't it? It's easier to do a job correctly when you know how and why you are to do it. Paul followed his normal writing pattern by telling us what to do (doctrine) in the first three chapters. Now, in the next three, he will give us the how and why (practical advice). Paul tells us to walk worthy in verse 1. How? By exhibiting three qualities: lowliness (true humility), meekness (gentle control), and forbearance (patience with others). Why? As believers, we share seven *ones* in Christ. Did you see them in verses 4-6? Meditate on them today.
Are you walking worthy? Do you exhibit the three qualities? Examine the things believers have in common in Christ and walk in unity with others.

thursday • Ephesians 4:11-16

DIGGING DEEPER • When was the last time you were called a *baby*? It usually means someone is saying you're behaving immaturely. That's what Paul is calling the believers in verse 14 if they haven't grown up spiritually. Spiritual children are often doctrinally insecure and fall when someone comes along with false teaching. It is plain in verse 14 that spiritual unity and spiritual maturity are closely linked. God gives each believer certain gifts and abilities to be used for His service in *the work of the ministry ...and edifying the body*. We each have things we can do that others cannot. Unity in the faith needs to be our goal for God's honor and glory.
Are you a spiritual baby? Make a list of what you can do today to mature in the faith. Today, use your gifts and abilities to help someone else mature.

friday • Ephesians 4:17-24

DIGGING DEEPER • Choices: We make them every day. Some may seem unimportant; however, they could make a great deal of difference to someone else. In this passage Paul gives us two choices. We can either live as unbelievers or as believers living in the truth. The choice is ours. Romans 1:21-25 explains what happens to those who choose to stay in the world. Those *in Christ* will want to put off the old man, renew their mind, and put on the new man. These issues are covered more in Romans 6:6 and Colossians 3:10. The Christian life is likened to stripping off the dirty clothes of a sinful past and putting on the snowy white robes of Christ's righteousness.
What do you need to *put off* and *put on* today?

saturday • Ephesians 4:25-32

DIGGING DEEPER • What kind of people do you like to hang out with? Hopefully, people who will help you in your walk with the Lord and warn you when you head in the wrong direction. Paul points out four important traits to work on in our lives. These are also good qualities to look for in a friend: 1) Are we truthful (v. 25)? 2) How do we control anger (v. 26)? 3) Do we steal (v. 28)? 4) What is our speech like (v. 29)? We all need to work on these traits. Paul closes this chapter with some positive characteristics that should be a mark of all believers: kindness, a tender heart, and forgiveness.
Closely examine one of these traits in your life. What can you do to improve it? Do you look for friends who will help your spiritual walk?

What do husbands and wives, children and parents, slaves and masters, and you and I have in common? Submission! Some people don't like to be under authority. Paul will help us understand the hows and whys of being in Christ and the unity we can have with others.

Week 8

prayer focus for this week

theQuestion theAnswer

What is the writer saying?

How Can I apply this to my life?

sunday • Ephesians 5:1-7

Q

A

DIGGING DEEPER · Guys, did you have a secret place that you went when you wanted to be alone so you could make some key decisions? Gals, did you have a dress-up box when you were little? Was there a place you could go to let your imagination run wild and pretend to be whatever you wanted to be? Paul is telling us that, when we are aware of who we are doctrinally in Christ (vv. 1-3), we need to live in a way worthy of that calling. This relationship makes it possible to live on a different level than the unsaved can know – a life ordered by love. Because *God is love*, believers emulating Him will live a life that manifests that same love. If we are true followers of Christ, our desire should be to avoid the pagan pitfalls listed here and live a life pleasing to the Lord. **Whom are you imitating or following? List two pitfalls you will put off today.**

monday • Ephesians 5:8-14

DIGGING DEEPER • Have you ever been afraid of something (real or imagined) in the dark? Maybe it was a nightmare, strange noises, or you were in a strange place. The dark can be scary! In Christ, we are to be lights in the world (Matthew 5:14). You should live so others will see and be drawn to the light. We are not to have fellowship with darkness, but show others how they can come to the light (John 1:9). Paul points out some contrasts between the condition of the unbeliever and the believer. The believer has two responsibilities regarding sin. First, he must have no part in it. Second, he is to reprove such behavior in others.

Exercise 1 John 1:9 to get rid of all sin in your own life. Now be a light for the Lord and draw someone who is in the dark to Him.

tuesday • Ephesians 5:15-21

DIGGING DEEPER • What does it mean to walk *circumspectly*? It means to walk *carefully* or *accurately* when making decisions. We are to be wise in the choices we make everyday as to how we walk in the Lord (v. 15 and Psalm 19:7). Paul gives us some *dos* and *don'ts*. Some of the *dos* are: *do* redeem the time (v. 16), *do* understand what God's will is (v. 17), and *do* be filled with the Spirit (v. 18). How are we to accomplish these three huge tasks? Verses 19-21 tell us first to enjoy music with other believers and in our own hearts. Then always give thanks for everything God has done. Finally, we are to submit to one another.

How are you walking? What are you doing to redeem the time? What can you do to understand God's will and be filled with the Holy Spirit?

wednesday • Ephesians 5:22-33

Q
A

DIGGING DEEPER • Are you thinking you can skip this passage since it doesn't apply to you yet? You're probably not going to get married for several years. Look again. What characteristics should you look for in a mate? Paul would suggest that you ladies start looking for a man who will love you as Christ loved the church and who would be willing to die for you. Guys, you should begin looking for a wife who will lovingly submit to your authority and show you reverence and respect. When a husband practices such Christ-like love, willing submission on the part of the wife is not difficult. God intends marriage to be a picture to the world of the relationship between Christ and the church. **Make a list of the characteristics you will look for in a mate. Follow each with a Scripture reference. What qualities do you need to develop?**

thursday • Ephesians 6:1-9

Q
A

DIGGING DEEPER • If you were raised in a Christian home, verse 1 was probably the first verse you memorized. It still applies today. Study Exodus 20:12 to see the origin of this verse and the promise it carries. From children's obedience, Paul moves to slaves' obedience. You may not think this applies to you, but when you are employed, it will. You are to submit to an employer as you would the Lord Jesus. In all these basic relationships, we are to understand that no matter who we serve (spouse, parent, or employer) we are ultimately serving Christ. **Look again at Exodus 20:12 and examine the only promise God gave in the Ten Commandments! To whom are you submitting? Do one thing today that you know Christ wants you to do to serve Him!**

friday • Ephesians 6:10-17

DIGGING DEEPER • Do you have all your armor in place? Step in front of God's spiritual mirror (His Word) to see what you look like. Paul explains that the battle is real and no true soldier of Jesus Christ can expect to be immune from enemy attacks. Remember he is writing from jail and fully armored soldiers are in plain view. We are to put on real (spiritual) armor so that we will be able to stand firm against a very real enemy. When examining each piece of armor Paul describes, notice there is nothing protecting the back. God expects us to face our enemy, to stand firm, and to be strong. We are always to be prepared.
Do you have all your armor on? Which piece can you strengthen to be able to stand up to and fight a real enemy who ultimately wants to destroy you?

saturday • Ephesians 6:18-24

DIGGING DEEPER • When we are in the middle of a spiritual battle, what is the most important weapon we have to fight the enemy? PRAYER! Our enemy makes it the most difficult weapon to use because he knows it is the most powerful. Paul tells us to pray with *prayers* and *supplications*. What's the difference? Prayer is the general term, what we're to do without ceasing (1 Thessalonians 5:17). Supplications are specific requests (Psalm 119:170). Mighty things happen when God's people pray specifically. Read the prayers of Moses in Exodus 33:12-23, of Joshua in Joshua 10:12-15, of Solomon in 1 Kings 3:4-15, and of Hezekiah in Isaiah 37:14-38.
Get ready to go to battle today with the knowledge of how to use the best weapon at your disposal. Read the powerful prayers listed above.

Week 9

Have you ever heard the saying, "The only thing unchangeable is the fact that everything changes"? Changes happen in our lives constantly. People die. New obstacles arise. Fear, deception, and battles rage. In this week's reading, you will discover how you can be successful in overcoming the inevitable changes of _life_.

prayer focus for this week

the Question
the Answer

What is the writer saying?

How Can I apply this to my life?

sunday • Joshua 1:1-11

Q
A

DIGGING DEEPER • We must remain changeless in our focus upon God's unchanging Word. At some point, someone we love and look up to will die. Moses died and Joshua was very nervous about the future. He no doubt wondered about God's plan for his life. The Lord reassured Joshua of His unchanging plan, presence, and precepts. Four times God told Joshua, _Be strong and of good courage_. The book of Joshua is a picture of our Christian life. Saved from the bondage of sin (like Israel was delivered from Egypt), we are called upon by God to possess all the spiritual blessings God has for us in the future. There will be battles, troubles, and obstacles. But as we meditate on and faithfully obey God's Word, He will not fail us (v. 5) and we will have good success (v. 8).
When death strikes, how can you best adjust? What role does faith play?

monday • Joshua 2:1-11

DIGGING DEEPER • God answers honest questions. Sometimes we have honest questions and that is okay because the truth can handle questions. As the spies met with Rahab, the harlot, she revealed military intelligence of enemy morale (vv. 9-11). Her help was God's answer to Joshua. When she said, *the LORD your God, He is God* (v. 11), it would appear that she became a believer. Rahab lied to protect the two spies. We need to learn to distinguish between what the Bible reports and what it recommends, what it records and what it requires. Scripture reports she lied, and requires, *Thou shalt not bear false witness*. While it is obvious that Rahab lied by the record of what happened, God's Word is in no way condoning lying.
In military campaigns is it right to deceive the enemy? How does this square with God's commandments?

tuesday • Joshua 2:12-24

DIGGING DEEPER • The promises of God are sure, but it helps when we FEEL sure of God's promises. Joshua's spies made a deal with the new believer, Rahab. Israel would spare her family if she kept their secret and dropped a scarlet cord out her window. Israelite soldiers would see the cord and not attack her home. The spies escaped capture and reported to General Joshua. In verses 23-24, it is easy to sense Joshua's relief and reassurance in God's promise to deliver their enemies into their hands. He now felt absolutely sure. When we are honestly seeking to be sure, God often gives us the evidence we need. Consider Acts 1:3, *Jesus showed Himself alive after His passion by many infallible proofs*.
Have you ever been unsure about God's promises? When you are unsure about God's promises, what will you do from now on?

wednesday • Joshua 3:1-17

DIGGING DEEPER · The exercise of God's power on our behalf is often governed by our submission to Him. God instructed Joshua to move the whole camp to the edge of the river. Shittim was less than seven miles from the Jordan. Why move two to three million people such a short distance? They camped and watched the Jordan River at flood stage for three days. With all their livestock and supplies, they realized how helpless they were to try to cross it alone. God would have to make a way. The Ark of the Covenant represented God's holiness. In effect, the Lord was teaching: *"Obey Me, and I will make a way. Believe in Me and all things are possible."* Once again, God reassures victory (vv. 7, 10).
When you face an impossible situation, what should you do? What was God trying to teach His people in this situation?

thursday • Joshua 4:1-14

DIGGING DEEPER · When we are with friends late at night in places we shouldn't be, sometimes it is so easy to forget God. The greatest enemy of our faith may be our forgetfulness. Memories of God's great works in our lives tend to fade. We need something to help us remember. Spiritual memorials in our lives remind us to walk with the Lord and pass on to others a reverence for His name (vv. 6-7). Memorials are like signposts that help us stay on the right road. They help us remember the goodness and greatness of God. When our hearts remember the Lord, we will not stray far from His side. The Israelites stacked stones in the middle of the Jordan and in the camp as memorials to the miracle of God drying up the river.
What kinds of memorials can you erect in your life to help you stay plugged in with God? How can you share these with others?

friday • Joshua 4:15-5:1

DIGGING DEEPER • Memorials remind us that total obedience is the key to God's blessing. The priests are a perfect example. They were told to go down into the water—they went. They were told to stay in the middle of the dry river—they did. They were told to come up into the Promised Land—they came. They showed wholehearted obedience. Memorials will remind us of God's blessings in the time when we turned to Him in obedience to His Word. The tenth day of the first month (v. 19), exactly forty years before, Israel began to prepare for the first Passover in Egypt. Forty years of wilderness living had taught this generation to trust and obey the Lord.
In what ways do you trust and obey the Lord? Is it wholehearted? What is one area that you could do better at trusting and obeying?

saturday • Joshua 5:2-15

DIGGING DEEPER • If we are going to fight and win the battles of life, it is important to consecrate ourselves to God. *Consecrate* means to set apart or dedicate for sacred use. Military intelligence may have suggested, since the Canaanites were caught off guard with the miraculous Jordan crossing, "Strike now!" Earthly circumstances are not always a good indicator of the will of God. *Wait and consecrate* was God's plan. Before the battle of Jericho, Israel needed to celebrate the Passover. To do that, they needed to be circumcised. This act represented consecration, which can be seen as a mark of maturity. After they consecrated themselves, God increased His blessings.
Would you consider yourself *wholly consecrated* to the Lord? Is there in an area in your life that you need to surrender today? Will you do it?

Do you believe it's possible for time to be extended or turned back? This week's reading is incredible! God uses marching feet and trumpets to topple huge walls. He stops the solar system for a man, rains hail to kill His enemies, gets upset with a thief, and rewards long-term faith. Stay with it and see how He pulls it off.

Week 10

prayer focus for this week

the Question
the Answer

What is the writer saying?

How Can I apply this to my life?

sunday • Joshua 6:1-11

Q
A

DIGGING DEEPER • When we honor God with obedience, God honors us with victory. The strength of Jericho's walls no doubt made the Lord's words surprising. *"See"* (v. 2) was a definite call to view things with the eyes of faith, not reason. It was *trust and obey* to *believe and receive*. God-honoring obedience complies with the details of God's Word. They did exactly what God said to do—nothing more, nothing less. It probably seemed bizarre—a silent attacking force marching circles around the city walls. However, the Lord always honors honest and true faith in Him and His Word. It is noted they marched *before the ark of the Lord* and *before the Lord* (vv. 7-8). When we walk in faith, God's presence is always with us. Acting in faith sometimes means looking stupid to others, but in the end, we win.

How can you do God's will when you feel stupid doing it? What will result?

monday • Joshua 6:12-27

DIGGING DEEPER · Many start out in strict obedience to God wanting to do right. Then our determination fizzles. We end up disobedient rather than obedient. When we are taunted, sneered at, and pressured, we compromise. It happens; and when it does, we lose. Imagine the taunts and sneers coming from the defenders on top of the walls of Jericho. God probably wanted Israel to march seven days in silence (v. 10) to keep them from being tempted to compromise and disobey. They might have wanted to whisper, *"This is crazy! Joshua is nuts!"* Then they would have lost. God-honoring obedience does not yield to pressure but complies until the very end. Wholehearted obedience brought the walls down.
Which is best: Starting well, finishing well, or both? How can you counteract the effects of peer pressure? Why is faith important for victory?

tuesday • Joshua 7:1-13

DIGGING DEEPER · Secret sins ultimately result in open trouble. God moved, and Israel defeated Jericho. Only one problem—Achan stole goods that should have been destroyed. Some wonder how a God of love could order the total destruction of a city. They forget a God of holiness judges sin. After receiving four generations of mercy (Genesis 15:16), all the –"ites" of Canaan were now hopelessly depraved and had to be taken out. God used Israelite armies instead of earthquakes or disease to do the job. But there are dangers here. Israel got cocky. Joshua got careless or overconfident. And because of Achan's secret sin, at the next battle, the good guys got pounded! That's the consequences of secret sin (vv. 12-13).
Do you have secret sin in your life? How can your secret sin hinder the group? How does God feel about sin?

wednesday • Joshua 7:14-26

Q

A

DIGGING DEEPER • A little private investigator work revealed the culprit who had cost Israel the battle at Ai. The elimination went from tribe (Judah) to family (Zarhite) to household (Zabdi) to individual (Achan). Achan delayed until it was impossible to conceal his guilt any longer. He confessed. Probably the heart problem of Achan began years earlier with dissatisfaction. Remember that Jericho was the first opportunity to see the spoils of war. Maybe Achan considered himself a classy guy. Wearing the same robe for forty years in the wilderness was not cool (Deuteronomy 29:5). Was the Babylonian garment like a *Gucci or Armani?* Later, God gives Israel the spoils. But here, perhaps as a test, nothing could be taken. Achan (v. 24) is Hebrew for *trouble*. Secret sin not only destroyed him but also his family. **How can you avoid the *valley of trouble?* How do you affect your group?**

thursday • Joshua 10:1-14

Q

A

DIGGING DEEPER • Standing with God is the key to living a life of victory. When we stand with God it will not be long before we learn the same lessons as Joshua. You will face satanic opposition. Five kings formed a coalition to fight against Israel. Ever feel *ganged up on* by the devil? When we stand with God, we will discover God keeps His promises. If we do our *best*, and trust Him with the *rest*, the end result will be blessed. Joshua called an all-night march extending more than 20 miles and ascending more than 4,000 feet in elevation that would have even tired out a modern Special Forces unit. When we stand with God, we will receive His supernatural resources. God used hailstones and stopped the clock of the solar system (see also Isaiah 38:7-8) to give victory to His people. **How do your duties and God's promises fit? How can you stand with God?**

friday • Joshua 11:16-23

DIGGING DEEPER • The godly life is a *battleground* not a *playground*. Those who lay hold on God's promises are those who hang tough through God's battles. The conquest of the Promised Land was not short and sweet; it was a long, grueling, demanding process (v. 18). Our commitment to live for God will be tested by the Lord. God caused every people in Palestine (except the Gibeonites) to hate Israel. This is what theologians call *judicial hardening*. God *gives them up* to their sin, confirms them in rebellion, and by it leads them to destruction. It is hard, but hanging tough with God enables us to defeat even our greatest enemies—the *"Anakim"* were giants (v. 21). *The bigger they are the harder they fall.*
What are some of the battles you have faced in your Christian life? How did God help you through? Is there any battle too big for God?

saturday • Joshua 14:5-15

DIGGING DEEPER • Ideal faith clings to God's Word regardless of the passing of time. For forty-five years, Caleb stood for God with courage, maintained a willingness to stand alone, went against the majority, and trusted God. He did not flinch but *wholly followed the LORD* (v. 8). Caleb's anchor was God's Word: *the LORD said (spake)* ... (vv. 6, 10, 12). Faith that anchors itself on God's Word will not be disappointed. False teachers say, *"If you have enough faith, you will get a miracle."* However, the Bible teaches that it is not great faith that is required, but rather faith in a great God! Jesus said all it takes is faith as small as a mustard seed. It is not how much faith you have, but rather what you have your faith in that is important. Caleb believed and then he went out to possess the land.
What characterizes ideal faith? How can you develop a faith like Caleb's?

Why is it so easy to bounce between being a good Christian on Sunday and being a wimpy Christian during the week? As Joshua closes his book and his life, he gives some straight up advice on how to live straight for God. Stay devoted in your reading: His advice is a critical element in faithful living.

Week 11

prayer focus for this week

the Question
the Answer

What is the writer saying?

How can I apply this to my life?

sunday • Joshua 20:1-9

Q

A

DIGGING DEEPER • The *"cities of refuge"* were designed to give sanctuary to those who committed manslaughter (unpremeditated killing). If an axe head slipped off its handle and killed a man (even though it was an accident), the victim's relatives could hunt down the woodsman and retaliate by killing him! This could happen UNLESS the woodsman ran into a city of refuge. Deuteronomy 19:1-13 best summarizes Moses's teaching on refuge. God's justice is pure enough to always punish the guilty but fair enough to always protect the innocent. In order to live, the manslayer was forced to reside inside the city limits until the death of the current high priest. Only the blood of the blood-shedder or an acceptable substitute could atone. Death is the only ransom that can satisfy the claims of God's justice.
Why is God called our refuge? How did God satisfy His own justice?

monday • Joshua 21:43-22:9

DIGGING DEEPER • General Joshua charged the two-and-a-half tribes that had settled on the east of the Jordan River to send their fighting men into Canaan to assist in the battle (1:12-18). They were vigilant, faithful, and successful. We can applaud them for this; however, it was not God's original intention for them to settle anywhere else than the Promised Land. Often God will let us have what we ask in order to show us that He (not we) knows what's best. Tracing the tribe's history that settled east of Jordan, we find they were the first to fall prey to future invading armies. Lack of faith, dissatisfaction with God's plan and will, and maybe even selfishness, ended up costing much more than following the Lord.
What can we learn from those who settled for *second best*? How do you feel when what God wants is different from what you want?

tuesday • Joshua 23:1-8

DIGGING DEEPER • When we act like one of the crowd, God still holds us accountable. Joshua wants the next generation to be faithful. It was *"because of you"* (v. 3), meaning the Israelites, that God defeated their enemies. Israel was faithful: That's why they won! They refused to be tarnished by Canaan's culture. Our culture believes in fate, horoscopes, luck, or the good side of *the force*. These are no different than Canaanite stone idols. Today, the world rubs a crystal for power. Back then they worshipped an idol for power. Going along with the crowd will influence us to disobey the Lord. Since you have to answer for what you do, it doesn't matter if everybody is doing it! Forget about being sociable. Stick with God.
How does culture influence you? Is there something that this culture has influenced you to do, say, or believe that is contrary to the Bible?

wednesday • Joshua 23:9-16

DIGGING DEEPER • To win spiritual battles, we need God as the focus of our life. When we love Him, we will trust and obey Him. The crowd and our culture will always try to dampen our love for the Lord. The world constantly places demands on our time, energy, love, loyalty, and life. There is not enough room in one's heart for the Lord AND the crowd. James 4:4 reads, *whosoever… will be a friend of the world is the enemy of God*. Joshua is warning the Israelites of the consequences of living like the world. If we let the crowd cause us to forget the good hand of God, disobey His precious Word, dampen our love for Him, and be separated from His protection, we will get burned (v. 16)! Be careful to always love the Lord.
Is your love and obedience stronger or weaker than a year ago? Why does obedience motivated by love please the Lord?

thursday • Joshua 24:1-13

DIGGING DEEPER • To stay on spiritual track, we must remember what we were and what we would still be if it were not for the grace of God. Joshua gives a review of Israel's history up to that point. It is incorrect to look upon Biblical characters like Abraham as if they deserved God's grace. Before God spoke to him, Abraham was a vile, idolatrous pagan. Isaac, Jacob, Esau, Moses, and Aaron all had their shortcomings. Disobedience, wandering, and death marked the wilderness years, but Joshua barely mentions their failure (v. 7d). Grace is totally of God. Note the many times the Lord refers to Himself in the first person: *I took, I gave, I sent, I brought*. When we look back on our lives, if we honestly have walked with Him, we will see that God's grace guided and supplied.
What is needed to thrive spiritually? Define grace and what it means to you.

friday • Joshua 24:14-24

DIGGING DEEPER · Because of what God has so graciously done for us, it is time for us to make our choice for Him. There are a lot of pleasurable things in the world to lure us away from our commitment to God. A solid choice for God means more than lip service. It means we are willing to put away the things that come between the Lord and us. Anything that hinders our walk with God is an idol. It seems Joshua already knew some in the congregation were slipping (*put away the gods among you)* (vv. 14, 23). We should realize, even after God has been good to us, if we turn on Him, He may still bring chastisement in our lives (v. 20)! Serving God is not a game. It should be done in sincerity and truth, not lightly, but with determination just like Joshua.
Have you ever found yourself slipping from the Lord? What specific things can you do in your life to stay strong in the Lord?

saturday • Joshua 24:25-33

DIGGING DEEPER · Remembering the victorious example of Joshua, we must daily choose to serve the Lord. The book closes with the obituary of Joshua. What a life of faithfulness! Joshua was an average man who chose to make himself available to God. He was great because he made godly choices. He took no short cuts. He dogged his way through the conquest by fighting and trusting all the way. Yes, it's true—he needed a lot of encouragement; but his faith was solid and grew with each trial and victory. Joshua set up stones of remembrance three times: 1) at Gilgal, to remember the Jordan crossing, 2) at Ebal, to remember the mercy of God, and 3) at Shechem, to remember the people's commitment to serve the Lord. It was at Shechem that God first promised the land to Abraham.
How will others remember you? Are you seeking to impact others?

What do you do if you are stuck on an island or are in a church with people who only want to cause trouble? Or what do you do with a thief who is on the run? How could you handle these problems when you're in prison yourself?! That's where Paul was when he wrote the books of Titus and Philemon. Don't miss it.

prayer focus for this week

the Question
the Answer

What is the writer saying?

How Can I apply this to my life?

sunday • Titus 1:1-9

Q
A

DIGGING DEEPER • Paul writes to a friend of his named Titus. In the past, Paul had helped Titus grow as a Christian, and now Titus was helping others grow. Titus lived on an island called Crete. There were a number of churches on that island that needed help. Paul's job was to help these churches get organized and appoint men to lead. Verses 6-9 give a list of qualities that are expected in church leaders. The key is verse nine. *Any church is just one generation away from extinction*. All you have to do, is fail to pass on what God has taught you. It's the job of every person in the church to pass it on and help others grow.
After listening to God's Word, are you committed to putting it into practice? Who can you help today to grow spiritually by sharing God's Word?

monday • Titus 1:10-16

DIGGING DEEPER • The churches in Crete needed help because there were unruly and deceptive individuals in the church. Men in these churches were teaching things that were false. They were stirring up trouble because they wanted the power to do what they wanted. Were there really men like this in the church? YES! It even happens today. That's why it's essential to know God's Word and practice it. Truth is either going to be taught and spread, or error will. It was Titus' job to train elders in every city. That way when error tried to creep in, they could recognize it and could deal with it. The church must follow *godly* men who follow Christ.

Are you living an unruly life? Does your lifestyle resemble one that is in submission to the Lord? Do you willingly submit to God's Word or choose to follow your own desires?

tuesday • Titus 2:1-10

DIGGING DEEPER • Paul has something to say to everybody in the church. He divided people into five groups that covered everyone. There were older men, older women, younger women, younger men, and bondservants (workers). First, he encourages them all to speak sound doctrine—that's what the Bible says. When others teach false doctrine, it's easy to get soft or stop standing firm. Paul wanted Titus to stay strong, even though he wouldn't be very popular. Verse seven is the key. It's been said, your talk talks, and *your walk talks, but your walk talks louder than your talk talks*—live it in front of others! Actions will always speak louder than words! We must live what we believe. If we don't live it, we really don't believe it.

Are there any actions in your life that are not consistent with what you believe? Think of one, now what are you going to do to change it?

wednesday • Titus 2:11-3:3

DIGGING DEEPER • Verses 11-14 show a pattern for us to grow in Christ. God's grace came to us (people who were sinners), and He lovingly saved us (v.11). We were unable to save ourselves. As a result of this grace we are now empowered to live godly lives. Sin should no longer master us and we should now live… (v. 12) … looking (v. 13) for His glorious appearing. His salvation should produce a change in attitude, appetite, ambition, and action. Verses 3:1-2 share a few ways we can grow spiritually; whereas, the next verse (v. 3) describes the kind of life we had before we were saved. The emptiness is nothing we should want to go back to.

Name two ungodly things or worldly lusts that trouble you. With God's help, will you endeavor to refuse to yield to them today? Will you demonstrate your love by changing?

thursday • Titus 3:4-15

DIGGING DEEPER • Paul begins by reminding them (as he did in 2:11) that their salvation is a gift from God. Their good works had nothing to do with it. The Holy Spirit had transformed (changed) them. Even their daily walk is something that He empowered by His mercy. Today, this same transforming power enables us to live for Him and maintain good works. He's done it all. There is no longer any excuse for us to live like we used to. In chapter 1, Paul encourages Titus not to argue with those men who were teaching things that were false. Just stick to doing right! Don't give up! Never quit living for God. You will never regret it.

Do you have a friend (or friends) who often discourages you from living for the Lord? Who would be a positive influence to help you live for God? Will you seek their help today and avoid those who discourage you?

friday • Philemon 1-9

DIGGING DEEPER • Paul calls himself a prisoner "of" Jesus Christ, even though this letter was written while he was *in* a prison cell in Rome (v. 1). There is a difference and it's *who* holds him captive. Paul goes on to commend his friend, Philemon, for his Christian character, but in verses 8 and 9, Paul has something serious to talk to him about. He wants Philemon to respond because of their love for each other. We'll check that out tomorrow. Romans 6:16 says we are slaves, or in this case, captives, to someone. We can be slaves to our selfishness or to Christ. One way leads to life, and the other to death. The choice is yours … but not the consequences.

Who has control over your life? List an area that you need to surrender to Christ. Will you yield it to Him today?

saturday • Philemon 10-25

DIGGING DEEPER • Enter Onesimus, a runaway slave, who belonged to Paul's friend, Philemon. The bad news is that not only did Onesimus run away, but in the process stole something of Philemon's. It so happens (under divine guidance), Onesimus and Paul meet and Paul has the privilege of leading him to Christ. Paul knows stealing from Philemon was wrong, and knows Onesimus must go back and make it right. Paul sends him back to Philemon with this letter offering to pay back what Onesimus stole. Paul asks Philemon for another favor… to forgive Onesimus. He is no longer an unprofitable slave, but is now a profitable brother in Christ (v. 16).

Is there someone who has wronged you that you need to forgive? Is there someone who you treat badly, but should be treated as a fellow believer?

The "Book It" program used in many schools encourages young people to read books. The reader is given a reward according to the number of pages read. This week, you will be given the promise of blessing simply for reading, hearing, and keeping the words of the Book of Revelation. Ready for rewards? Read on!

Week 13

prayer focus for this week

the Question
the Answer

What is the writer saying?

How Can I apply this to my life?

sunday • Revelation 1:1-8

Q

A

DIGGING DEEPER · How do you feel when someone lets you in on a secret? Maybe you were kept in suspense for a long time and then, finally, he revealed his plans to you. There's usually a high that goes with it. The word *revelation* means *unveiling*. As John records the events God revealed to him, he unveiled both God's message about the future and about His Messenger—Jesus Christ. The first truth that the Apostle John unveils to the seven churches of Asia is that Jesus Christ, the One Who was, is, and is to come, will return to earth for every eye to see. Now that's a HIGH!

Are you ready for His return? If Jesus Christ were to come today, are you prepared to meet Him?

monday • Revelation 1:9-16

DIGGING DEEPER • Have you ever seen something that "blew your mind"? Maybe it was an unbelievable stunt or an inconceivable performance. Did you ever try to describe it to a friend? While John was on the Island of Patmos, he saw and recorded a vision of the glorified Christ. After standing in awe of the Son of Man, he used the best words he could find to describe the majesty of the One whom he beheld. He compared the voice of the One he saw to the sound of trumpets. He compared His eyes to a burning fire, His feet to brass, His words to a sword, and His face to the brightness of the sun. That's enough to "blow anyone's mind."

What is your view of Jesus Christ? Is He the most awesome person you have ever met? What will you tell your friends about Him today?

tuesday • Revelation 1:17-20

DIGGING DEEPER • "But I just can't do it!" The task may seem overwhelming. "This is too much for me to handle." When we reach this point, it is always great when someone puts his arm around us and says, "Calm down, I'm here for you." John faced an overwhelming experience (an experience that literally caused him to fall on his face). However, in the midst of his dramatic situation, the Lord lifted him up and let him know that everything was all right. The Lord comforted John by revealing Himself to him and giving him a task to perform. Encouragement, especially from the Lord or a fellow believer, is always welcomed when we have a difficult task to perform. It helps us realize we can accomplish whatever we've been asked to do.

Will you allow the Lord to be your comfort in your next overwhelming situation? See Him for who He is and trust Him to lead you well.

wednesday • Revelation 2:1-7

Q

A

DIGGING DEEPER • Sunday: Sunday school, morning service, puppet practice, evening service; Monday: visitation; Tuesday: mission service; Wednesday: teen group… The attitude of apathy had invaded the church at Ephesus. They were performing many good deeds and did not tolerate false teaching, but they had forgotten the reason for service. Sure, they did much to further the kingdom of God, but it was all done out of habit and ritual. They were serving the Lord because it was expected of them, not because they loved Christ. **So, why do you do your Quiet Time? Why are you involved with Christian Service projects? Is it because you *ought to* or is it because you *want to*? Spend some time right now in prayer and fall in love with Jesus Christ again. It will help you fulfill what you need to do with the proper attitude.**

thursday • Revelation 2:8-11

Q

A

DIGGING DEEPER • Have you ever watched a news reporter describing the devastation caused by a hurricane? Every year, meteorologists predict where hurricanes will hit. Yet, as you watch the news reports, someone who has lost everything is bound to say something like, "This is where we live. We are not leaving. We will just rebuild and prepare for the next one." The church at Smyrna had suffered persecution and was told that more persecution was on the way. Yet, they stayed faithful to Christ despite their current persecution and the promise of even more to come. Faith that is strong even in difficult times is something worth having. **How faithful are you to Christ? Do you stay true when others laugh at you for being a Christian? Will you stay faithful knowing that persecution may come in the future? Determine today that nothing will shake your faith.**

friday • Revelation 2:12-17

Q

A

DIGGING DEEPER • "You scratch my back and I'll scratch yours." This was the mentality of the church at Pergamos. The Lord let them know that He was aware they lived in a difficult city. He was proud of this church that stayed faithful to His name, even to the point of death. However, He called into question their compromise. They had allowed false teaching to abide in the church. The Lord was calling them to separate themselves from things that He hated. If they did not repent, God promised that He would judge the false teachers, and the church would be guilty by association. **From whom do you need to separate yourself? Have you allowed worldly entertainment to have a place in your life? Today is the day to repent of the sin and surrender your heart wholly to the Lord.**

saturday • Revelation 2:18-29

Q

A

DIGGING DEEPER • A purebred golden retriever is 100 percent golden retriever. In order to stay pure, the golden retriever must only mate with another golden retriever. As the fiery eyes of the Lord searched the church in Thyatira, He found a small blemish that was causing a rather large impurity. A single member of their church had been allowed to teach her false doctrine and had led many members into error. Her teachings had rendered the church impure. The Lord was going to cut out the imperfection. He encouraged the church to separate from her and to hold fast to that which is right. *A little leaven, leaveneth the whole lump* (1 Corinthians 5:6). **What imperfection do you need to separate yourself from in order to remain pure?**

Three more letters to Asian churches, John's description of Jesus Christ and the activity in His throne room, the perfect picture of worship, and the four Horsemen of the Apocalypse are all waiting for you to discover. Read the Word of God carefully this week. His truths are fascinating.

Week 14

prayer focus for this week

the Question
the Answer

What is the writer saying?

How Can I apply this to my life?

sunday • Revelation 3:1-6

Q
A

DIGGING DEEPER · For a plant to thrive, it must receive proper care. Water, the right amount of heat and light, soil, and nutrients are all necessary for growth. If a plant is deprived of any one of these requirements, it will wither and die. The church at Sardis was in the *withering* stages. The Lord told them to cultivate the little bit of life that was left in the church. He told them that if the dying church did not strengthen itself, it would ultimately die. In fact, if they did not take the appropriate steps necessary to rejuvenate the church, the Lord would come upon it like a thief with judgment.

How healthy is your spiritual life? Are you dying on the vine? Will you make a decision today to cultivate your Christian life with the water of the Word, the light of God's illumination, and the soil of your church?

monday • Revelation 3:7-13

DIGGING DEEPER • "I just can't do it anymore." Have these words ever run through your brain? Maybe you were trying to get that last pull-up done in gym class or maybe you were refusing to give into that sin that constantly assaults you. The Lord realized that the church at Philadelphia had little strength. Nevertheless, they had clung to the Lord even when they were weak, refusing to bail out on God. He promised to keep them "from the hour of temptation" (v. 10). Making the decision to let go of the rope, drop off the pull-up bar, or yield to temptation may seem like the easy way to avoid a difficult situation, but in every case, you lose. Hang on! Allow God to be your strength. He will help you win.
Will you trust Him today? Will you keep His Word so He can keep you from temptation? Victory can be yours.

tuesday • Revelation 3:14-22

DIGGING DEEPER • "He thinks it's all about him." "She thinks the world revolves around her." Have you ever met people like that? They are difficult to tolerate and even harder to convince of the truth. The church at Laodicea was cocky. They were sure they already had everything they needed to survive. No one could tell them anything. However, the Lord viewed this arrogant church differently. He let them know very bluntly that they were despicable. He made it very clear that their lifestyle sickened Him so much that He wanted to vomit. Can you imagine someone saying that about you? Does your life nauseate God? Are you so self-absorbed that you can't hear Him knocking at your door?
Will you give up your selfish ideals and open the door of your heart so Jesus Christ can come in and fellowship with you today?

wednesday • Revelation 4:1-11

DIGGING DEEPER · Think of majesty. Think of splendor. Think of glorification. God brought the Apostle John into Heaven and allowed him to view the future. Limited by words, John tries to describe the awesomeness of the Throne Room of God. He describes, as best he can, four unusual creatures having six wings each. It is their continuous job to give glory and honor to God. The praise of the creatures triggers the praise of the elders and the Throne Room echoes in undying honor to God. Everything God created offers praise to God except one thing… man. Isn't it time that we learned to praise Him for all He has done?

How much do you praise the Lord? The creatures do nothing but praise Him. Today, give God the glory and honor He deserves.

thursday • Revelation 5:1-7

DIGGING DEEPER · Have you ever faced an impossible task? When you get into a situation where no one can help you, life can get a little frustrating. John described a situation that was so frustrating it brought tears to his eyes. No one was worthy to open the book God held in His hand. As John wept over the situation, one of the elders revealed that the Lion of the tribe of Judah was worthy to open the book. However, when John turned around to see this "Lion," he saw a Lamb who looked as if He had been slain. John saw the only worthy One, Jesus Christ, take the book from the hand of God. We appropriately sing, *Worthy is the Lamb!*

How do you see Jesus Christ? He is the Lion of the tribe of Judah and the Lamb of God who takes away the sin of the world. Will you worship the Lamb because He is King?

friday • Revelation 5:8-14

DIGGING DEEPER • What is your definition of worship? The Apostle John describes sincere worship of Jesus Christ in this chapter. Worship is *giving something its worth.* The elders who were the redeemed (and thus human) sang praises to Jesus Christ simply because He was worthy to open the book. Notice, however, that their worship was not limited to singing (vv. 12-13). They, in unison, said that Jesus Christ was worthy *to receive power and riches, and wisdom and strength, and honor and glory and blessing.* The Lamb that was slain is alive forevermore and is worthy to receive endless praise.
How much do you praise the Lord? Besides singing worship songs, how will you worship Jesus Christ? Will you commit to worshipping Him with your speech today?

saturday • Revelation 6:1-8

DIGGING DEEPER • In the 1990s, the Four Horsemen of the World Wrestling Federation (WWF) had a reputation for inflicting pain on other wrestlers. However, those four never inflicted as much pain and sorrow on the human race as the Four Horsemen of the Apocalypse will. The rider of the white horse carries a bow without arrows and represents conquest through a political takeover. The red horse is a symbol of war and will steal peace from the earth. With the arrival of the black horse comes famine. The inflated price of wheat and barley reveal the high level of demand and the low level of supply. The pale horse brings death. Those who have not accepted Christ will face these coming judgments.
Are you prepared to meet Christ? Which of your friends will you warn of these future events?

No Hollywood horror film can compare to the description of destruction, terror, and chaos found in the pages of Revelation. The evil creatures from the bottomless pit are unleashed on the earth, but some people will be protected from this bedlam. Find out who is spared as you read this week's passages.

prayer focus for this week

the Question
the Answer

What is the writer saying?

How Can I apply this to my life?

sunday • Revelation 6:9-17

Q

A

DIGGING DEEPER • If you have ever wondered what the Tribulation period will be like, John gives a vivid description. Jesus Christ opens the fifth seal and John views the souls of countless martyrs longing for some type of vindication. When they were given white robes, they were told to rest until other martyrs had fulfilled their calling. When the sixth seal is opened, the natural structure of the universe is jolted out of alignment. The earth suffers a great earthquake. The sun refuses to give forth its light. The moon appears as blood. The stars fall to the earth with catastrophic effects. The mighty men of the earth will seek death as an alternative to the wrath that is to come. Jesus Christ possesses limitless power. **How can you give Him the proper respect today? Pray for someone that's not saved, so they can avoid this coming judgment.**

monday • Revelation 7:1-8

DIGGING DEEPER • Let's take a break! It's as if the writer of Revelation is given time off from death and destruction. Between the sixth and seventh seal, John gives his readers a breath of fresh air. He reports that 144,000 men (Revelation 14:1, 4) are sealed with a mark. Once they are marked, God Himself protects them. The Bible is very clear that these 144,000 are all of Hebrew descent. They are preserved for the purpose of evangelism. Some teach that only these 144,000 will go to Heaven. Others teach that anyone who accepts Christ after the Rapture will be part of this 144,000. According to the Bible, these Hebrew witnesses will win others to Christ during the Tribulation period. God will protect His children.
How has God protected you this week? Are you His child and worthy of His protection? Can you think of a friend or loved one who needs protection?

tuesday • Revelation 7:9-17

DIGGING DEEPER • Do you ever desire to do great things for God? Have you ever wished that your life could impact many for Christ? Because of the sealing of the witnesses (vv. 7:1-8), John sees an innumerable host of people standing before the throne of God. In verse 14, we are told that they are people who have come out of the Great Tribulation as children of God. Because the 144,000 witnesses do their job, many people in the Tribulation period will come to know Christ. Wow! What an impact! You can make an impact as well. The 144,000 witnesses simply fulfill the task that God had purposed them to do. If God has saved you, your task is to be a witness for Him before the Rapture.
How many people will come to Christ because of your willingness to fulfill your task? How will you be a witness for Christ? Who's on your list today?

wednesday • Revelation 8:1-13

Q
A

DIGGING DEEPER • Before a tornado hits, the wind may die down and the air may become very still. This is what is known as "the calm before the storm." As the final seal is opened, an eerie silence covers Heaven. After thirty minutes of tranquility, seven angels prepare to sound their trumpets. The first angel uses hail and fire to destroy one-third of all vegetation on the earth. The second angel turns one-third of the oceans into blood. This causes the death of one-third of the sea creatures and the destruction of one-third of the ships. The third angel attacks the fresh water with bitter poison. The fourth angel attacks the heavenly lights and they cease giving forth their light. But the worst is yet to come.
If you knew a great tornado was coming, would you not warn others to seek protection? Others need protection from the Great Tribulation.

thursday • Revelation 9:1-12

Q
A

DIGGING DEEPER • After reading today's passage, one might feel as though he had seen a horror film. When the bottomless pit is unlocked, a swarm of evil creatures comes out of the pit. These hideous locusts are described as having the face of a man but the body of a horse. They have long hair like a woman and teeth like a lion. They can fly and when they do, it sounds like an army of chariots going into battle. The worst part of these creatures is the sting of their tails. John reported that when these locusts sting a man, the pain will be with him for five months and he will be unable to die. The name of their king, Abaddon, means *destroyer*. What a true description of their task!
Will you fear God now with reverential awe? Or will you fear God later in sheer terror?

friday • Revelation 9:13-21

Q
A

DIGGING DEEPER • As if the locust creatures of Revelation 9:1-12 are not enough, the sixth angel sounds his trumpet and ushers in tribulation woe number two. An army of 200 million is unleashed on the earth with one purpose in mind—to kill one-third of all men. The "horses" they travel on are dragon-like creatures. They have heads like a lion but can breathe out fire and brimstone. They have tails like a snake, but each tail has a head that can cause pain as well. These creatures will kill one-third of all mankind, but like Pharaoh of Egypt, the remaining two-thirds of mankind will refuse to repent of their wickedness and will still be determined to worship false idols that can neither hear nor deliver.
Has God been trying to get your attention? Is there a sin you need to surrender? What will God have to do to get your attention?

saturday • Revelation 10:1-11

Q
A

DIGGING DEEPER • Six of the seven angels have sounded their trumpets. Tribulation woe number three is yet to take place. An angel who is holding a little scroll descends from Heaven. As his thunderous voice is heard, John begins to write down the actions of each thunder. Before he can write, he is told not to write about the thunders. Obviously, there is more to the Tribulation than man is privileged to know. After the angel speaks, John is told to "eat up" (read and internalize) the book that the angel has. It is sweet to the taste because it is the Word of God, yet it is bitter because it is a judgment upon the earth. John would have to prophesy the words of this book to the world.
How strong is your faith in God? When you don't have all the answers, will you still trust in Him?

God sends two witnesses to Jerusalem to proclaim His name, a giant earthquake rocks the city, and the Tribulation is visited in an overview in this week's quiet time. Failing to read this week's Scripture would leave a giant gap in your knowledge of the future, not to mention the reward of blessing promised (1:3).

Week 16

prayer focus for this week

the Question
the Answer

What is the writer saying?

How can I apply this to my life?

sunday • Revelation 11:1-12

Q
A

DIGGING DEEPER • Do people hate you because you are a Christian? John records the actions of two witnesses that God sends to earth. During their 1,260 days of prophecy, God gives them the power to breathe fire from their mouth and destroy any would-be attackers. Because they perform similar miracles to those of Elijah and Moses, it is possible that they are these same two Old Testament saints. When the 1,260 days of prophecy are past, the Lord will allow them to be killed. During the three days that they are dead, the people of earth will send gifts to one another with rejoicing over the death of these witnesses. They refuse to bury their bodies because they hate them so much. After three days, they come back to life. **Why does the world hate Christians so much? How will you love your enemy today?**

monday • Revelation 11:13-19

DIGGING DEEPER · Have you ever experienced an earthquake? Maybe you have seen the devastation caused by one. As the second woe ends and the two witnesses ascend back into Heaven, a great earthquake rocks the city of Jerusalem killing seven thousand men and causing even unbelievers to glorify God. As the seventh angel sounds his trumpet, the triumph of Christ is announced and the twenty-four elders worship God. As the heavens open and the ark is revealed, the earth experiences lightning, thunder, voices, an earthquake, and great hail. All reveal the power of God Almighty. An earthquake should remind us that God is more powerful than we are. The twenty-four elders remind us to worship Him. **How will you worship Christ today? Will you praise Him for His power? Will you share the news of God's power with someone else today?**

tuesday • Revelation 12:1-9

DIGGING DEEPER · "And she brought forth her firstborn son, and wrapped him in swaddling clothes, and laid him in a manger; …" (Luke 2:7). Revelation gives a different view of the birth of Christ. The woman represents Israel. The twelve stars are the twelve tribes of Israel. The child is Jesus Christ. The great red dragon is a picture of Satan who has a desire to destroy Jesus. Verse 4 records the fact that Satan took one-third of the angels (stars) with him when he was cast from Heaven. From the time of Christ's birth, Satan has desired to destroy Him, but God has a master plan and He is in control. **Do you trust the Lord even when His ways are confusing? How will you show Him that you trust Him today? List some of the ways that God has been faithful to you. Then, thank Him for His faithfulness.**

wednesday • Revelation 12:10-17

Q
A

DIGGING DEEPER · When someone accuses you of doing wrong, how do you react? Satan spends his time in the Throne Room of God making accusations against Christians. After a war with Michael, the archangel, Satan is kicked out of Heaven and confined to the earth. Because he is confined to earth, he begins to persecute the *seed of the woman*. However, God protects His children by providing a place of refuge in the wilderness for a time (1 year) and times (2 years) and half a time (1/2 year). When Satan realizes that Israel is protected, he angrily prepares to go to war with her. The Lord is the Savior. Satan is the accuser. **Will you live in victory because of His salvation or in defeat because of Satan's accusations? What will you do today to defeat Satan or your selfish desires?**

thursday • Revelation 13:1-10

Q
A

DIGGING DEEPER · How do you feel when you find out something is phony? If someone pretends to be one thing and turns out to be something different, does that frustrate you? Satan (the dragon) will give power to the Beast (Antichrist) to "rise up" (resurrect) from the dead, to rule for three-and-a-half years and to be worshipped by many. During his rule, he will openly speak out against Jesus Christ. He will make war with the saints and defeat them. Any unsaved person at this time will worship the Antichrist. Satan is a phony. He tries to imitate Jesus' actions while He was on the earth. When we ally ourselves with Satan, we choose to be friends with a fake. The choice is ours … but the consequence is not. **This week, how can you cast off the phony works of the devil? Will you join teams with a "phony christ" or with the Real One?**

friday • Revelation 13:11-18

DIGGING DEEPER • The Godhead is made up of three persons—the Father (God), the Son (Jesus Christ), and the Spirit (Holy Spirit). Satan, the phony counterfeiter, will try to mimic this unique union—the dragon (Satan) as "the father," the Beast (the Antichrist) as "the son," and the second Beast (the False Prophet) as "the spirit." This false prophet will direct worship to the Antichrist. With his deceptive miracles, he will persuade many to worship the Beast. Those who refuse will be killed. He will connect the economic structure of the earth with loyalty to the Antichrist. Anyone who does not receive the mark of the Beast ("666") will not be able to buy or sell.

How can you be sure you do not fall for Satan's counterfeits? Make a commitment today to study that which is true so you will not fall for a fake.

saturday • Revelation 14:1-7

DIGGING DEEPER • If you were drowning in a pool, and someone rescued you, what would your opinion of him be? Would you have a high respect for him? Would you tell others of his actions? In chapter 14 (the Tribulation in review), Jesus Christ appears on the Temple Mount with the 144,000 witnesses who have been redeemed. These witnesses are probably virgin males who are strongly tied to Christ or at least faithfully married men who have not been defiled by immorality (Hebrews 13:4). After this appearance of Christ, an angel, having the "everlasting gospel," instructs the inhabitants of the earth to fear, glorify, and worship God.

Have you received God's salvation? Have you been rescued from the cesspool of sin? If you have, how will you fear, glorify, and worship God today?

Some unbelievable sights are just ahead in Scripture. The final seven vial judgments are poured out on the earth in a "grand finale" style. The blood of millions of soldiers will flow four feet deep in a valley 200 miles in length. An evil woman, a weird beast... but Christ claims the victory.

Week 17

prayer focus for this week

the Question the Answer

What is the writer saying?

How Can I apply this to my life?

sunday • Revelation 14:8-13

Q
A

DIGGING DEEPER • Would you join a team if you knew for sure that the team would lose? If defeat were guaranteed, how anxious would you be to get involved? The Bible records the fact that the Antichrist and his government (Babylon) will be defeated. During the Tribulation, anyone who joins the Antichrist by receiving his mark will get severe, undiluted judgment. On the other hand, an angel announces that the children of God who die in the Tribulation are blessed. It will be better for them to die than to finish out the rest of the Tribulation. By doing the works of Satan today, you are joining his team. But remember, he will ultimately be defeated.

What will you do today to show that you are on God's team? It's not too late to do some recruiting from the other side. After all, no one wants to be a loser!

monday • Revelation 14:14-20

DIGGING DEEPER · Have you ever been grounded or lost some important privilege because of disobedience? At the time, it probably felt like the worst thing in the world. Your parents have the right and authority to punish your improper behavior. Today, John records the punishment of those who disobey God. The "reaping" in this passage is referring to judgment. The nations who rise up against God will be destroyed. A winepress is used to crush grapes to make juice. When God crushes these nations, their blood will flow over four feet deep for 200 miles. The punishment God delivers will be swift and just. Why would anyone want to go through this time of judgment when deliverance is available? **If you are a born again believer, will you spend time right now thanking God for sparing you from His wrath? Pray for someone who's unsaved.**

tuesday • Revelation 15:1-8

DIGGING DEEPER · Have you ever watched a television show that ended with the words "To be continued"? The entire next week you waited in anticipation to see what would happen. After reading Revelation 10, it seems like there was a break in the action. In chapters 11-14, John took a break from recording judgments and turned to speak the prophecy of the *little book* that he *ate up* in chapter 10. In chapter 15, he finally allows the judgments "to be continued." After the Tribulation saints sing a worship song to Christ, seven angels are given a vial (bowl) judgment, which they will pour out on the earth. Watch out, these are powerful! **Knowing that God will one day judge His enemies, whom will you warn? Instead of being frustrated with the arrogance of sinful man, trust that one day God will settle the score.**

wednesday • Revelation 16:1-12

Q

A

DIGGING DEEPER • Have you ever known someone who does not learn from his mistakes? The followers of the Beast are so foolish that even unparalleled judgment cannot get them to repent from their sinful ways. Festering sores plague the inhabitants of earth. The entire sea clots up, like the blood of a dead man, killing all sea creatures. The third angel turns the fresh water into blood. The fourth angel uses the sun to burn men and scorches them with a great heat. The fifth angel causes darkness to cover the earth and the sixth angel dries up the great Euphrates River. Through all this, the followers of the Beast *repented not of their deeds* (v. 11). Oh, the blindness, stubbornness, and rebellion that sin creates. **How far does God have to go to get your attention? Will you commit to repenting of your sin quickly so God does not have to discipline you?**

thursday • Revelation 16:13-21

Q

A

DIGGING DEEPER • Anyone who has ever watched a fireworks display knows that the best part is the end. The *grand finale* is the climax of an unforgettable display of power. Much like fireworks, the seventh vial judgment ends with a gigantic *bang*. The great sores, the water turning to blood, the scorching sun, the darkness and the dried up river are just the beginning. Using a giant earthquake, God caps off His powerful display. The earthquake destroys every city, flattens every mountain, and wipes out every island. To top off the earthquake, 100-pound hailstones fall, destroying more life on earth. In the midst of all the terror, anyone who watches for the return of Christ is blessed (v. 15). **Do you anticipate Christ's return? What can you do today to be ready? Do you have a friend that needs to hear some "Good News"? Share it today.**

friday • Revelation 17:1-8

DIGGING DEEPER · Did you ever see something that totally amazed you? *Ripley's Believe It or Not* is famous for bizarre scenes. After the seven vial judgments, John is taken into the wilderness by an angel so he can view an unbelievable judgment. When John first sees the beast and the woman, he is stunned. The royally dressed woman is partnered with all types of evil. She represents Babylon, the governmental system of the Antichrist. She is responsible for the death of many saints. The beast that she rides "was, and is not, and yet is." In other words, he was alive, he died, but he came back to life. Satan is deceptive. You must know the real thing so you do not fall for his powerful trick. **Will you commit today to study God's Word for five more minutes each day so you can know the truth better? Why not review a memory verse, too?**

saturday • Revelation 17:9-18

DIGGING DEEPER · It is easy when reading this passage to scratch your head and say, "I don't get it. It's too confusing." This passage contains a lot of imagery. The seven heads are really mountains and have kings. Each king represents a great world leader. The ten horns are ten kings who ally themselves with the beast in an attempt to conquer the Lamb of God. It is shown here by the many "waters" that the people groups of the earth will follow the beast. Despite the imagery, verse 14 presents the climax of the matter. This beast, with the people, and the kings of the earth try to make war with the Lamb of God and they are miserably defeated. Even the most powerful ruler on earth will one day kneel before Jehovah Sabbaoth. **How can you worship the King of kings today? You can start by bending the knee and acknowledging Him as Lord of lords and Kings of kings.**

Satan's destruction is in sight. The city of Babylon will fall this week. The birds of the earth will eat the carcasses of dead soldiers. The wedding of Jesus Christ and His bride takes place and Satan is bound for 1,000 years. Whether you are a guy or a girl, this week's quiet time has something for you. Don't miss out!

prayer focus for this week

the Question   What is the writer saying?
the Answer   How Can I apply this to my life?

sunday • Revelation 18:1-8

Q
A

DIGGING DEEPER • Have you ever met someone who thought he was *untouchable*? Maybe it was the principal's son at your school. His dad is in charge so he thinks he can break the rules and be fine. The great city of Babylon thought she was above the rules. She was wicked and filthy (v. 2). She caused others to be wicked as well (v. 3). She had gotten God's attention by the magnitude of her sin (v. 5). She thought she would never be judged (v. 7). The truth is she is going to reap all the evil judgment in one day (v. 8). God tells His people to separate from her or they would receive judgment as well. Judgment may seem delayed, but you can be sure it will come and will be complete. **Knowing that all sin will be judged, what evil practice or habit will you separate from today? Will you commit right now to do it?**

monday • Revelation 18:9-19

DIGGING DEEPER • *It all depends on whom you trust.* The kings of the earth, who had trusted their *security* to Babylon, cried because Babylon had fallen. The merchants of the earth, who had trusted their *wealth* to Babylon, cried because she had fallen. The shipmasters and sailors, who had trusted their *occupation* to Babylon, cried because she had fallen. It is interesting to note that the kings (v. 9), the merchants (v. 15), and the shipmasters (v. 17) all *stood afar off.* They allowed their beloved city, once she was destroyed, to go down by herself. They used her for their gain in good times but *stood afar off* when she burned. Satan can bring you prosperity, but it will be temporary and be assured, he will forsake you. **Will you decide today to trust in God alone? What can you do today to prove your loyalty to Jesus Christ?**

tuesday • Revelation 18:20-24

DIGGING DEEPER • All of your life you have probably been taught to be a good sport. When you won a game in little league, you probably had to shake hands with the other team. That mentality is tremendous and proper to have in sporting events; however, when Satan's team loses it should be reason for God's people to celebrate! Christians are told to rejoice because Babylon had fallen (v. 20). When she receives her just reward, it should be the cause of much rejoicing. No longer would jubilation fill her streets. She had shed the blood of prophets and saints and she would no longer be allowed to continue. Evil will not always prevail. *Vengeance is mine; I will repay, saith the Lord* (Romans 12:19). Praise the Lord! **How will you act today in a way that will make Satan lose? What action will you take that will damage Satan's attempts to control you?**

wednesday • Revelation 19:1-8

DIGGING DEEPER • Have you ever been to a wedding? Most weddings are joyous occasions. The bride has prepared herself for her groom. She is dressed in a clean, white dress. The guests at the wedding are joyful and singing the praises of the couple. In Revelation 19, we see the "marriage of the Lamb." The Bride of Christ had been given white clothes. No longer is she impure. She has prepared herself for her marriage to the Lamb. What a joyous occasion! The church is united with her Savior. Will you be part of this blessed arrangement? Only those who have accepted Christ will be part of the Bride of Christ. This is one wedding you will want to be part of. Find out all about it tomorrow. **Who will you tell today about this future ceremony? Who can you talk to today about accepting Christ?**

thursday • Revelation 19:9-16

DIGGING DEEPER • Have you ever been to a gathering when the President of the United States spoke? When the announcement, "Ladies and gentlemen, the President of the United States," is spoken, the crowd claps and cheers as the Commander-in- Chief enters the room. When the Lord comes back, the fanfare will dwarf the celebration of any world leader. Jesus will come riding on a white horse to judge and make war. His clothes will remind all of the blood that He shed for them. The armies of heaven will follow Him as He smites the nations with the Word of His mouth and begins to rule with an iron rod. He has this right because He is the King of kings and Lord of lords. **How much respect do you have for political leaders? How much more respect should you have for Jesus Christ?**

friday • Revelation 19:17-21

DIGGING DEEPER • When an animal dies in the wilderness, it doesn't take long for some type of vulture or scavenger animal to find the carcass and begin to feast. As the King of kings and Lord of lords arrives on the scene, an angel invites all the birds of the heavens to gather for a feast. Immediately, the Lord captures both the beast and the false prophet and casts them alive into a lake of fire. The armies that remain without their leader are killed by a few simple words from the Word of God. Every bird on the planet fills his belly with the flesh of the dead. What a gruesome scene! Satan's armies are destroyed by the words of God. It's the wedding feast of verse 9 or the feast of the fouls in verse 21; it's either eat, or be eaten.
Do you have enough respect for God's Word that you will read it daily? There are some that have not made the right choice. Will you help them?

saturday • Revelation 20:1-6

DIGGING DEEPER • "Okay everyone, take five." Such a phrase is common in show business. The actors are given a short five-minute break. Here in Revelation, it is as if God says, "Okay everyone, take one thousand" (years, that is). Since the first sin of Adam, the world has yet to have a break from the terrible reign of Satan. Finally, it comes. Satan is bound in the bottomless pit for a thousand years. During this time, Christians will reign with Christ on earth. The second death has no power over those who reign with Christ in the millennium. However, Satan will be allowed out of the pit for a short period of time (v. 3) after the millennium. He will attempt one last time to deceive people into following him in a revolt against God.
Which event will you be a part of: the first resurrection or the second death? Be sure today that the second death is not an option for you!

This week we will see Satan get his final shot to overthrow Jesus Christ. The old serpent will be cast into the lake of fire forever and ever. You will get a personal tour of your new home where God will rule and reign with His children. If you read the back of this book, you will see that we win. It's great being a winner!

Week 19

prayer focus for this week

the Question / the Answer

What is the writer saying?

How Can I apply this to my life?

sunday • Revelation 20:7-15

Q

A

DIGGING DEEPER • "Ok, I'll give you one more chance." Have you ever said this to someone? Maybe you have been arm-wrestling your little brother and he still thinks he can win. You know what the outcome will be, but to humor him, you give him one more shot. For reasons unknown to us, God allows Satan out of the bottomless pit long enough for him to gather an army to attempt a final overthrow of Christ. This time God simply causes the recruits to go down in flames. Finally, the devil is cast into the lake of fire and tormented forever. All the unsaved, both small and great, will be judged at the Great White Throne, and will be cast into the lake of fire where they will join Satan. The Bible says this is the second death.

Are you on the winning side? Who will you talk to about joining the winning side today?

monday • Revelation 21:1-8

DIGGING DEEPER · *In the beginning God created the heavens and the earth* (Genesis 1:1). *And I saw a new heaven and a new earth* (Revelation 21:1). A lot has happened between the first chapter of Genesis and the last chapter of Revelation. Now after the Tribulation and the millennium (1007 years), John sees the New Jerusalem come down out of Heaven. God decides that He is going to be with His people. In the New Jerusalem there will be no tears, no death, no sorrow, no crying, no pain, and everything will be new. On the other hand, the fearful, unbelieving, abominable, murderers, whoremongers, liars, etc, will suffer the second death. Quite a contrast! Have you chosen yet? **Those who follow God will inherit life with Him. Those who follow Satan will inherit death with him. What will you inherit at the end of time?**

tuesday • Revelation 21:9-16

DIGGING DEEPER · "What did it look like?" Has anyone ever asked you to describe something to them? John has the awesome task of describing the New Jerusalem to all men both in his time and in the future. The first thing that John reports about the New Jerusalem is that it contains the glory of God (v. 11). The light of the city is as bright as a pure jasper stone. A great wall with twelve gates surrounds the city. Each side has three gates and at each gate stands an angel. Above the top of each gate is written one of the names of the twelve tribes of Israel. As John measures the city, each side is the same length as the other. It is 1,500 miles on each side. A perfect cube… for a perfect city… for a perfect citizenry. **Can you imagine what God has in store for His children? If He tells us this much, imagine how much is beyond our comprehension?**

wednesday • Revelation 21:17-27

DIGGING DEEPER • Take a walk through a good jewelry store and the beauty of the jewels will amaze you. Find the most beautiful emerald. Now imagine that it is 1,500 miles long and 1,500 miles wide. Fifteen hundred miles is the size of the foundation of the New Jerusalem. Then multiply that one foundation by twelve because the city has twelve foundations. What a sight the city must be! Can you imagine one pearl that would fit a gate for a wall that is 216 feet high? All these precious gems are not even the best part of the New Jerusalem. The best part is the presence of God! Jesus is the temple (v. 22), light (v. 23), safety (v. 25) of it. It's the perfect place to live. **Will you thank the Lord for His future blessing? Will you live today in light of your future home?**

thursday • Revelation 22:1-7

DIGGING DEEPER • "So, how does it end?" Jesus Himself reminds the readers of Revelation about the promise of this book. The person who keeps the prophecy of this book is blessed. He begins our blessing prematurely by giving us a preview of Heaven. A river will proceed from God's throne. The Tree of Life will once again be available to man. It has the unique ability to bear twelve different fruits. The curse of the Garden of Eden will be lifted. He reminds us one more time that Heaven will have no darkness, and most importantly, God will reign forever and ever (v. 5). And, oh, by the way, it doesn't end. It's just the beginning of eternity! **Now that you know the rest of the story, how will you live in light of this knowledge? Does knowing that God will reign forever change your view of Him? How?**

friday • Revelation 22:8-15

DIGGING DEEPER • Many times e-mail messages will pop onto your screen with the request to forward it to all your friends. Here in Revelation, John was told by God to make sure he was not the one who broke the "chain letter." The letter of Revelation is about finished. Are you going to talk about it or shut the prophecy up? God told John not to shut up the prophecy because it could happen at any moment. The same is true today. The words of this prophecy need to be proclaimed to the whole earth. It is all about Jesus. When John tries to worship the angel, he is told to get off his face and worship God alone. Jesus is the Alpha and Omega and He will reward every man according to his works. How will you be rewarded? **Will you "shut-up" the words of this prophecy or will you help keep it going? Share the Gospel of the death, burial, and resurrection of Jesus!**

saturday • Revelation 22:16-21

DIGGING DEEPER • "It's perfect." Ok, so nothing in this world is perfect, right? Wrong! John gives two warnings to all mankind. The first is, *If any man shall add unto these things, God will add unto him the plagues….* The second is, *If any man shall take away from the words of the book of this prophecy, God shall take away his part out of the book of life.* Since this is the final book of the Bible, these statements can be made not only of this book, but also of the entire Bible. If you cannot add to it to make it better and you cannot take away something to make it better, then it is perfect. Even though we have the perfect Word of God, God desires to dwell with us, so He promises to return. To which our only response should be, *Even so, come, Lord Jesus.* **Are you living in light of His return? Do you anticipate seeing Jesus Christ?**

What can three hundred men who lap up water in the cup of their hands do for God? In this week's reading you'll find out. It's an up and down world at times, as we walk with the Lord. Sometimes we're up. Sometimes we're down. This is not cool from God's perspective. Learn how HOT to do it this week in Judges.

Week 20

prayer focus for this week

the Question the Answer

What is the writer saying?

How Can I apply this to my life?

sunday · Judges 2:1-12

Q

A

DIGGING DEEPER · It's important to note the difference in the three words *isolation, insulation,* and *participation*. While Joshua was alive, the Israelites practiced *isolation* from the enemy. They fought to destroy all of the wicked Canaanites. God warned them if they did not absolutely destroy the evil, it would infect them. However, once Joshua died the Israelites practiced *participation*. Perhaps they were tired of the long fight or got acquainted with the enemy between battles. Perhaps they just wanted to be liked. They became infected, and God was displeased. The New Testament tells us to practice *insulation* –in the world but not of it.

How can you influence your unbelieving friends? How can you keep your unbelieving friends from influencing you?

monday • Judges 2:13-23

DIGGING DEEPER • It is a whole lot easier to walk with God while we are around our spiritual leaders. But when we are with a crowd that is not acting right, it seems just as easy to act up with them and disobey the Lord. In the book of Judges, Israel is held up as a classic example of this pattern. The pattern looks like this: 1) Multiple times Israel gets with the crowd and sins. 2) God allows their enemies to beat the tar out of them. 3) Israel prays. 4) God sends a judge (a deliverer/leader). 5) As long as the judge is alive, Israel does okay. As soon as the judge dies, the cycle begins all over again. Because of sin, God stops empowering them to overcome their enemies. God gives the enemy the advantage so He can test His people's resolve and heart for Him. That was the problem: They had no heart for Him.
How do you act if your spiritual leaders are absent? Where's your heart?

tuesday • Judges 6:1-10

DIGGING DEEPER • In certain circumstances, what God will do is very predictable. When we sin, God will speak before He spanks. He will speak after He spanks. And He will spank again if we do not listen. Such is the book of Judges. The background is set for the Lord to send yet another judge to deliver Israel. Many times years of trouble follow disobedience (v. 1). *"Midian"* means *strife*. Living contrary to God's will produces a strife-filled, impoverished spirit, and in their case—bankruptcy and destitution. God was not about to let His people give their affections and worship to idols and continue to bless them with victory and prosperity. He warned them through Moses and Joshua. They still rebelled. He punished them. They still did not listen. They cried out. God sent a preacher to remind them of His love (v. 8).
Why does God speak before He spanks? What is the role of preachers?

wednesday • Judges 6:11-24

DIGGING DEEPER • The Angel of the Lord calls Gideon a *man of valor*, yet we see him scared to thresh his wheat in the open for fear of the Midianites. Things have been going badly for so long he questions the truth of the angel's statement, *The Lord is with you*. He shows disbelief in the old stories about Egypt, Moses, Joshua, and the miracles. Disobedience sprouts doubts! Yet Gideon is willing to hear Him out *if* the angel gives a sign. Rather than the outward appearance, the LORD looks at the heart. Gideon's heart looked good. After the angel vaporizes his food offering, Gideon realizes Israel's God is real. Being assured he won't die, Gideon built an altar and named it *Jehovah-shalom* meaning *the Lord sends peace*.
Does God only pick great people to be leaders? Are you open to God using you? What questions would you ask God if He chose you to be a leader?

thursday • Judges 6:25-40

DIGGING DEEPER • In the Bible idolatry is severely condemned. Idolatry is a horrible sin that leads to more horrible sin. The altar of Baal and the *"grove"* (think shade trees here) next to it was a place of satanic worship and perverted sex ceremonies. Altar boys and girls were there for the *worshippers* to engage in homosexual, heterosexual, and other sexual depravity. It speaks of the heart condition of the men who wanted to kill Gideon for throwing down Baal's altar, cutting up the grove, and burning it. God demands first place in our lives. Though filled with fear, Gideon got the job done. His dad told the angry men, if Baal IS a god, let him defend himself. If God intended us to use fleeces (sheepskins) to find His will, there would be more people than just Gideon using that method in the Bible.
Name some modern-day idols. How can God have first place in your life?

friday • Judges 7:1-14

DIGGING DEEPER • Jerubbaal means *let Baal plead*. It's the nickname Gideon's dad gave him after Gideon smashed Baal's altar. Baal was the god of the Midianites. It appeared he was about to avenge himself on Gideon. Gideon called in the troops and 32,000 Israelite soldiers showed up. They faced the 135,000 well-trained and equipped Midianite military. Gideon set up camp next to the well of *"Harod"* meaning *trembling*. When God whittled Gideon's combat force down to three hundred men, the odds of winning seemed impossible. God told Gideon to descend down the hillside and spy on the Midianites. If he was afraid, he could take his servant Phurah. They obtained enemy morale intelligence that confirmed victory was in the bag. God gave the Midianites bad dreams, and they knew it was over.
How does God ease your fears? Why is it bad to think you can do it alone?

saturday • Judges 7-15-25

DIGGING DEEPER • Little is much, when God is in it. When Gideon heard the thoughts of the enemy, he knew without a doubt his three hundred men would defeat their 135,000 men. The battle would be won with clay pots with lamps inside them in one hand, and trumpets in the other hand. The Midianites changed their guards just after midnight, and, while their eyes were still adjusting to the darkness, they saw three different groups of one hundred soldiers. Gideon gave the signal and Israelites blew their trumpets and broke open the clay pots that had been shielding their lamps. The guards perceived a huge attack coming at them from three different directions. In all the commotion, the Midianites ran for their lives.
How have you seen God work when the odds were against you or someone you love? Take a moment to worship God for His power and plan.

Have you ever struggled with being double-minded? One day you may be living strong for God; and then the next, you're straying from the Lord. Samson is a classic example. At the end he pulled it out, but his whole life was a saga of flesh against Spirit. As you read, look at the details. They give heart condition clues.

Week 21

the Question the Answer

What is the writer saying?

How Can I apply this to my life?

sunday • Judges 8:22-35

Q

A

DIGGING DEEPER • It is often just after victory that some failure or stumbling occurs, so be very careful. Gideon knew better than to let the people make him a king, but he still created confusion when he asked for the spoil of gold earrings to make a gold ephod (high priest's vestment). The weight of the golden ephod was about fifty-four pounds. Israel was already given to idolatry so they started worshipping the thing! Gideon was not a priest (not even close). But something about an angel appearing to him, God speaking, and a miraculous victory, made him think he was somehow different, maybe better than his countrymen. Gideon fathered seventy sons with multiple wives. All of them but two die in chapter nine. Polygamy was tolerated but never approved by God in the Old Testament. **What should your response be when God helps you have a victory?**

monday • Judges 13:1-14

DIGGING DEEPER · Like a broken record *the children of Israel did evil again.* In Judges chapter 6 when Israel did evil, the Lord delivered them to the Midianites for seven years. Here the Philistines are given advantage over Israel for forty years. As they continue to disobey, God continues to heat up the punishment. You would think God's people would catch on. Samson was the next deliverer and verses 4-5 reveal what being a Nazarite involves: 1) a man set apart for God, 2) no strong drink, 3) no haircuts, 4) eat no unclean thing, and 5) no contact with dead bodies. However, there was a disconnect between what Samson was supposed to be and what he was. He eventually broke every part of his Nazarite vow. His parents' one-time pride in their son turned into utter disappointment.
What duties do you have that make your parents proud?

tuesday • Judges 13:15-14:4

DIGGING DEEPER · When Samson's parents were told about their son who would be a deliverer of Israel, they were humbled. Samson's dad, Manoah, asked the angel for his name. The angel answered, *Why askest … my name, seeing it is secret?* The Hebrew word translated *"secret"* is the same word translated *"wonderful"* in Isaiah 9:6. Isaiah's prophecy concerns the birth of Christ. This is a reason to believe *the angel of the Lord* in the Old Testament is a pre-incarnate (before being born) appearance of Jesus. Christ is from everlasting to everlasting! His name is *Wonderful.* The Lord blessed Samson but Samson yielded to his fleshly desires. His first mistake was who he married. Selection of a mate is one of the most important decisions one makes. So much hinges on that choice!
Why does it matter who you marry? How can you avoid fleshly decisions?

wednesday • Judges 14:5-20

DIGGING DEEPER • Samson had a drinking party to celebrate his marriage. While giving his marriage vows, he broke Nazarite vows (no strong drink). He killed a vicious lion because the Lord's spirit was on him. But returning later, he ate from the honeycomb of bees that had nested in the dead lion's bones (another vow—no contact with dead bodies). Like every double-minded person, Samson is a contradiction. God's spirit was on him, but he walked in the flesh. No man could beat him, but a nagging woman wore him down. The wife he thought he had to have ends up with his best friend (v. 20). He gave in, compromised, and violated his vows. There were moments of strength, but weak character soured his life for the Lord. **Why is it so important that your life and your commitments match? Ask God to strengthen you to help you fulfill commitments you have made.**

thursday • Judges 15:1-20

DIGGING DEEPER • Samson tried to visit his wife, but her father had given her to his best friend thinking Samson hated her because of what she did to him. The burning of the Philistines' fields was pure retaliation and angry revenge. No mention of the Lord here. The rest of Israel worried that the Philistines would take it out on them for Samson's behavior. They turned on him, tied him up, and brought him to the enemy. At this time, the Philistines ruled over Israel. What a sad state from what God intended for His people. Using the jawbone of a mule, Samson then killed one thousand Philistines. It was a good victory showing Israel's God was still there for them. God brought water in an unusual way to refresh his servant. Samson's life story was on again, off again with God. **What is consistency with God? What are the penalties for inconsistency?**

friday • Judges 16:1-17

DIGGING DEEPER • Proverbs 6:26 says, *"For by means of a whorish woman a man is brought to a piece of bread."* In other words, mess around with a promiscuous person, and you will be reduced to nothing and eaten for lunch. That's what happened to Samson. The chapter opens with Samson visiting a prostitute. He was by far the strongest man physically to have ever lived, but morally he was a weakling. If Samson lived in our day, he could easily win an Olympic gold medal. Oohs and ahhhs would be offered up because of his physique. He beats his enemies for a time, but his focus on sex was his undoing. A woman named Delilah brought the great Samson to a *piece of bread* and *ate him for lunch*. Loving this present world and disregarding God's commands ends in humiliation and defeat. **What is moral character? Why is it so important to remain sexually pure?**

saturday • Judges 16:18-17:6

DIGGING DEEPER • The *"lust of the eyes"* (1 John 2:16) is the desire to have that which is beyond the will of God. It is no surprise one of the consequences of Samson's lust was the gouging out of his eyes. His lover, Delilah, badgered him to reveal the secret of his strength. Weak-willed Samson told all. She cut his hair. His strength was gone. The enemy poked out his eyes, made him work like an ox at the mill, and made fun of him and His God. The saddest commentary is contained in v. 20. He did not know the Lord had departed from him. Samson redeemed himself in his dying act. Israel's problem was in worshipping other gods. Micah and his mother illustrate how idols had become commonplace. Everyone did his own thing, and God was ignored. **Why is Samson mentioned in the *"Hall of Faith"* (Hebrews 11)? What does this say about God's grace? What is an idol? How can you avoid idolatry?**

Have you ever heard the statement, "Prepare to meet thy God?" It's a quote from the prophet Amos. The context of the statement may surprise you. Hang in there in your reading. Knowing something about Amos and Obadiah will help you avoid judgment and receive God's blessings.

Week 22

prayer focus for this week

the**Question**
the**Answer**

What is the writer saying?

How Can I apply this to my life?

sunday • Amos 1:1-2; 3:1-7

Q
A

DIGGING DEEPER · After repeated offers of grace are spurned, God's wrath is a sure thing. Over and over again God has pleaded with Israel to get right, be right, and stay right. Israel continues to disobey. Our privilege and accountability are illustrated by the prophet: 1) Can two walk together unless they agree to go the same direction? 2) God, like the lion, roars only when there is a sure kill. 3) If we have no sin, why would the Lord be roaring against us? 4) If we live in sin, God's judgment will snare us. 5) Judgment will not catch us, unless we trigger it by disobedience. 6) Preachers sound the alarm and warn of approaching judgment. 7) God is the only One who brings calamity on us because of our sin.
Is there something in your life that another person could help you with? Are you in danger of discipline from the Lord?

monday • Amos 4:1-13

DIGGING DEEPER • Faking it is no good. God catches pretenders. The kine (cows) of Bashan are figurative of religious people whose hearts are wicked. They do all the right things (attend church, pay tithes, etc.) but it's all fake. They love being religious. At the same time they love being sinful. God will never accept this. He spoke FIVE times, but no one was listening: 1) famine, 2) drought, 3) blight, 4) pestilence, and 5) fiery trials. If our hearts are not right, God will try to get our attention with increasing intensity. If we will not heed Him, then *Prepare to meet thy God*. It's THAT serious! Resisting God's reproof leads to greater rebuke. Unless we heed God and stop pretending to be what we are not, there is deep trouble ahead. All the outward religion in the world will not help on judgment day.
We may be able to fool others, but is God ever duped? Why pretend?

tuesday • Amos 5:4-15

DIGGING DEEPER • In the face of impending judgment, God holds out the bright hope of relief to those who obey and believe. There is only one way to avoid God's judgment— *"Seek Him."* The Hebrew word translated *"seek"* means to pursue with care and diligence. The prophet begs us to seek the Lord (vv. 4, 6, 8, 14). Do we remember who we are dealing with? God is able to turn the threat of death into a bright morning of hope. But God is also able to turn a bright day of hope into a night of death and destruction. The Lord will not allow us to place anyone or anything between Him and us. Do not *"hate"* the pastor or spiritual leader who points out sin and the path of truth. Do not *"abhor"* (detest) true Christian friends who warn you about the consequences of sinful choices.
Has anyone warned you lately? Is there someone you need to warn?

wednesday • Amos 5:16-27

DIGGING DEEPER • For the ungodly *the day of the Lord* will be darkness. Those who do not seek God on *this day* will meet God on *that day*. The Day of the Lord is the terrible day of God. Israel believed the day would bring destruction for their enemies and blessing to them. Because of their wayward hearts, the exact opposite was true (v. 18)! They tried putting up a false façade, even tried running but to no avail. We may keep our outward life polished, shined, and clean. We may go to church each Sunday. We may know how to speak God-talk and Christian lingo. All the while we have a secret life of sin that we believe no one knows about. We may fool others, but we will never fool God. **How can you know God accepts your worship? Why can't God be fooled?**

thursday • Amos 8:1-12

DIGGING DEEPER • God strikes only when we make ourselves ripe for judgment. When we allow sin to decay our inner spirit and lives, we make ourselves ripe. Amos' vision of summer fruit in a basket pictures time that is running out. Privileges God bestowed on His children were misused. Invitations to repent were unheeded. Present warnings from the preacher were ignored. God said in effect, *"Enough! The game is over"* (v. 3)! When selfishness takes priority over our concern for others, we are ripe. When we ignore the ministering of God's Word, we make ourselves ripe for judgment. Time and again God's Word had been despised, ignored, trampled, and neglected. Therefore, God granted His people their desire. *You don't want to hear my word. Fine! I will not speak it* (v. 11). **Why is God's Word so precious? What happens when we obey or disobey?**

friday • Amos 9:8-15

DIGGIHG DEEPER • When it comes to God's purging of sin, the Lord's people receive no favors. Israel thought, *We are God's chosen people, He will overlook our sin.* Not so! They had become too wicked for God to stomach. Amos likens them to the heathen. *Your life is no different than that of a pagan.* History records the fact—sin does not pay. The Israelites were scattered the world over for more than two thousand years until the state of Israel was reborn in 1948. Beginning that year, the Jews started returning to the Promised Land. God is serious when it comes to purging our sin. When God is done whipping us, He gathers us up in His arms of love. No matter how deep our sin, the mercy of God is deeper still. In the future, Israel will once again play a major role in God's plan for the nations.
If God doesn't give up on Israel, do you think that He will give up on you?

saturday • Obadiah 15-21

DIGGIHG DEEPER • *What goes around comes around.* Obadiah was a prophet of God used to pronounce judgment on an enemy of Israel. The Edomites were particularly mean-spirited toward the Jews (v. 10). God allowed it for a while, but they took too much joy in beating down their brothers and plundering them. Now it was their turn. Obadiah also points out that God's people, the Jews, will be restored in the Lord's purpose for them. This prophecy is related to the last days and Christ's kingdom on earth. The house of Edom will be stubble. The house of Jacob (the Jews) will be a flame and a light. The fire of Jacob will devour the house of Edom. This one-chapter book is like a courtroom with arraignment, indictment, judgment, and sentence. Because of their actions, Edom is done forever!
How does the expression *you reap what you sow* apply here and to you?

Do you ever wish you could just start over? You can as we start this new gospel. We'll get a new perspective on who Jesus is and how He affected those around Him. This week we will learn about Jesus' first miracles and more about His deity. We can start fresh by asking, "Who is this Jesus?"

Week 23

prayer focus for this week

sunday • John 1:1-14

Q

A

DIGGING DEEPER • When you read "In the beginning," what was the first thing you thought of? Genesis 1:1, of course. God was already there when human history was first recorded. This passage explains that Jesus was the Creator of the world. John's Gospel presents Jesus in all His deity. He uses the terms *Word, Life,* and *Light* to reveal that Jesus is God. Then, to those who received Him (v. 12), He gave the power (the right) to become "sons of God." Do you find that amazing? We can become children of the Almighty God, by His will, of course, not ours (v. 13).

Are you a child of God? If you are not sure, talk to a leader or friend who can show you how. What are you willing to do for the Creator who wants to call you His child? Write down one thing and work on it this week.

monday • John 1:15-28

DIGGING DEEPER • Do you like riddles? There are many of them in Scripture. They make us think deeper than we normally think. The Apostle John, the author of this book, lets us see into the ministry and message of John the Baptist. People sent by the Pharisees asked him who he was. The Pharisees probably felt threatened by his ministry. John the Baptist responded with a riddle. He denied being the Messiah, Elijah, or the prophet but simply said he was *the voice* (Isaiah 40:3). His message clearly declares Christ's pre-existence as the Son of God and that His ministry would be full of grace and truth. **Think deeply about what John says about Jesus Christ. Who do people see in your ministry and message? Do something this week that enables you to share the Gospel with at least one other person.**

tuesday • John 1:29-42

DIGGING DEEPER • Have you ever known something and just couldn't keep it a secret? Maybe someone famous was coming to town and you were going to meet him. You would want everyone to know. That is the way John the Baptist is in these verses. God had revealed to him who Jesus was so John wasn't worried when his own followers left him to follow Jesus. If fact, he was happy (John 3:30). His follower Andrew, who later became one of Jesus' disciples, brought his brother Simon to meet Jesus, who Andrew claimed to be the Messiah. Andrew is known for introducing many people to Jesus (John 6:8-9; 12:22). **Do you know how to take another person through the Scriptures to show him that Jesus is God? Pray and ask God to reveal one person to you who you can introduce to Jesus Christ this week.**

wednesday • John 1:43-51

DIGGING DEEPER • What do you and your friends say about your cross-town rival on the night of the *big game*? It is usually a put down of one form or another—nothing flattering. That may have been how Nathanael considered the people from Nazareth. What a great example we see in Philip who, like Andrew, brought his friend Nathanael to meet Jesus. We don't know exactly what Nathanael was doing under the fig tree. Some scholars think he was meditating on Old Testament Scriptures or praying. It is clear that he quickly changed his mind about Jesus when Jesus told him where he had been. **What have you done about the person you asked God to reveal to you yesterday? Find a way today to talk to that person about Jesus.**

thursday • John 2:1-12

DIGGING DEEPER • Do you enjoy weddings? Most girls love them while most guys tolerate them. They are joyous occasions where the guests come to celebrate and encourage the new couple. The fact that Jesus chose a wedding to perform His first miracle shows us that He wasn't looking for recognition. If He were, wouldn't He perform the miracle in the temple or another public place with many people as witnesses? Also, look closely at what He did. He bypassed the whole process of growing the grapes and making them into wine. This miracle proves His ability to create with the appearance of age. This is the first of seven signs (miracles) that John records to convince us to believe in the Lord Jesus Christ and His deity. **What do you think about Jesus now? Write down one thing God taught you in today's passage and meditate on it.**

friday • John 2:13-25

DIGGING DEEPER • If you were in the temple that day, who would you be? Would you be a merchant, selling animals to those coming to make sacrifices for Passover? Maybe you'd be a banker *helping* people change their money to be able to pay for things. Both groups were greedy in their dealings and were very upset when this *new guy* came in disrupting things. Perhaps you'd be one member of the multitude there to celebrate Passover. They were probably puzzled about what was going on, but enjoyed the miracles. Even the disciples were a little confused. They were still learning who this Jesus was. They would remember these things after the Resurrection and it would strengthen their faith (John 12:16).
Whom do you relate to in today's passage? What is one thing you can do today to become a better disciple of Jesus? Do it.

saturday • John 3:1-12

DIGGING DEEPER • If you were a recognized religious authority, a teacher of the Law, and part of the Sanhedrin, why would you want to speak privately with Jesus after dark? Maybe it's because you are supposed to be the religious expert and don't want others to see you asking questions. Jesus patiently explained the spiritual second birth to Nicodemus, illustrating it with the wind. John mentions Nicodemus three times in this gospel so we can witness the progression of his faith. It is hard to believe that the first person to hear John 3:16 (from the Lord Himself) does not respond positively. We are not told what happens, but in John 7:50 Nicodemus defends Jesus against charges made by the Sanhedrin. Then, in John 19:38-39, Nicodemus stands with Joseph to care for Jesus' body after the crucifixion.
Where are you in your progression of faith? Take the next step!

Do people know you are a disciple of Jesus Christ because of your love for others and your faithfulness in obeying His Word? This week you will find people who knew Scripture, knew their place, and took God at His Word. You'll see Jesus ignore social codes and show real concern for people whom others hated.

prayer focus for this week

the Question
the Answer

What is the writer saying?

How Can I apply this to my life?

sunday • John 3:13-24

Q
A

DIGGING DEEPER · How much of the Old Testament do you know? Jesus understood that Nicodemus knew the Old Testament extensively. Therefore, He related the Exodus story in Numbers 21 to him. Read it. It's about complaining, rebellion, death, snakes, and surviving! In the end, the people were required to believe and look at something in faith. Jesus relates this story to His upcoming sacrifice on the cross as an example of how future generations will have to look forward in faith to the cross for salvation. Today we look back to the cross and must believe and receive by faith what Jesus has already provided.

Look back and truly thank Jesus for all He did for you on the cross. Read the passage in Numbers 21 and see how all of Scripture works together, even when written hundreds of years apart.

monday • John 3:25-36

DIGGING DEEPER • What are you best at when it comes to athletics or academics? Imagine you held the world record in that activity. What happens next? After several years, someone else will come along and break your record. Are you sad? Of course not. John the Baptist was probably one of the greatest men who ever lived. However, he knew who he was in comparison to the Lord Jesus Christ. Jesus was from Heaven and, by nature, was superior to him. God used John (and is still using him) to point many to Jesus. John was glad when more people followed Jesus than him. In verse 36, John gives a clear statement about what it means to be saved. Make sure you understand it; then share it with someone.
Pointing people to Jesus is the thing that matters most in life. Whom will you point to the Lord Jesus Christ today?

tuesday • John 4:1-15

DIGGING DEEPER • Jesus was not *politically correct* in His day. Most Jewish people did not associate with Samaritans because they were considered half-breeds. Also, in that culture, men didn't talk to women they didn't know. Jesus ignored the social code of His day and asked this woman for a drink of water. Why? We know from the miracles He's already performed that He could have provided for Himself. However, He knew this woman couldn't. She needed what only He could provide. Note that He used something she could relate to—*water*— to introduce and explain spiritual truth to her. Notice that she was interested in hearing more. The Lord always blesses those who genuinely seek Him.
What can you use to explain spiritual truth to someone? Ask the Lord to give you an opportunity today to share His truth with that person.

wednesday • John 4:16-30

DIGGING DEEPER • When someone is telling you things you don't want to hear, what do you do? Changing the subject is a popular deflection technique. The Samaritan woman used that method when she brought up the issue of where to worship (which was a major point of contention between the Jews and Samaritans). Jesus reveals that it is not the location but the heart attitude with which you come to God that's important (Psalm 24:4). What do you think the people of the town thought when the woman returned claiming that a man told her everything she'd done? She then wondered if this One could be the Messiah.

Is there a group of people you wouldn't approach with the Gospel? Get over it! Where do you worship? You can worship right now where you are!

thursday • John 4:31-42

DIGGING DEEPER • Do you live on a farm? Have you ever planted a garden? If you have, you know that when it's time for harvest it is crucial to get the crop in quickly before it rains. That is what Jesus is trying to get the disciples to consider. Instead, they worried about food as the people from the town were coming out to see Him. Jesus shares another principle with them that compares the known (or natural) with the spiritual. With the Gospel, not everyone gets to do the harvesting. Some will plant, some will water, some will cultivate, and others will bring in the harvest. In this case, the disciples got to do the harvesting.

Are you willing to skip a meal to share the Gospel with someone? Are you planting, watering, cultivating, or harvesting the Gospel today?

friday • John 4:43-54

DIGGING DEEPER · Are you willing to take God at His Word? How often have we seen God work in a mysterious way, and then later begin to second guess or explain it away? It's very easy to do and it is one of Satan's favorite tactics. He wants to get our focus off our Almighty God and onto something else. Notice the man didn't appeal to his royal position, or defend himself in light of Jesus' charge of wanting to see a sign, but he humbly in faith, appealed to Jesus to save his dying son. What a demonstration of Jesus' power! Cana was approximately twenty miles from Capernaum. We see that Jesus was as capable of healing the child from a distance as He was standing at his bedside. We can take God at His Word. **Claim by faith something God has told you in His Word. Consider memory work, witnessing, truthfulness, and faithfulness to name a few, and do it.**

saturday • John 5:1-14

DIGGING DEEPER · How many people do you know who cling to a false hope, or a false religion built on the traditions of men rather than the Word of God? It is popular today to believe in angels. It's interesting to observe that in today's passage, an angel was supposed to stir the pool and the next person in was believed to be healed. Note that it didn't say any person ever was healed. This type of healing is not found anywhere else in Scripture. Jesus had compassion on this one man and gave him a command, which he followed. The man was clear in his testimony to the Jews as to why he was disobeying a Sabbath law. The one who healed him from his disease of thirty-eight years had told him to do it. Wouldn't you? **Do what Jesus has told you to do. Share the truth; be a light to someone living in darkness. Obey the Word God has spoken to your heart.**

Do you always follow the rules? It's interesting to notice that Jesus didn't always follow man's rules. Being God, He had a good reason: He is the Ruler. This week we'll get a detailed look at Jesus feeding the five thousand and how the people wanted to follow the rules and be cared for physically but not spiritually.

Week 25

prayer focus for this week

the Question
the Answer

What is the writer saying?

How Can I apply this to my life?

sunday • John 5:15-27

Q
A

DIGGING DEEPER • Have you ever played a game with someone who didn't follow the rules? It's irritating, isn't it? That's what the Pharisees thought about Jesus. He wasn't following the rules that had been laid out by the *religious rulers* throughout the centuries. If only they knew to Whom they were talking. Jesus healed a man on the Sabbath, and claimed to be equal with God. Jesus Christ also declared His commitment to doing the Father's will, and made it clear that one cannot have a valid faith in God the Father apart from a faith in Jesus, the Son of God. The key is a relationship with the Ruler, not just obedience to the rules.

Whose rules are you following? What is one thing you can do today to show your love and commitment to Him?

monday • John 5:28-38

DIGGING DEEPER · What do you do when you want to prove a point to someone? You can argue the points yourself, but it's always impressive to bring in other witnesses to verify what you're saying. Jesus presents the Jews with five witnesses to His claim of deity. He is the first witness as to His deity. Second, John the Baptist is a witness. Jesus' miracles are number three. When John the Baptist doubted in prison, Jesus let His works assure John that He really was the Messiah. His Father is the fourth witness at His baptism, transfiguration, and Triumphal Entry. The fifth witness is Scripture (vv. 39-47). Unbelief is a powerful foe, but five irrefutable, reliable sources should be sufficient to verify His authenticity.
Are you a witness for the Lord Jesus? Share what the Lord has recently done for you or is teaching you in your quiet time with at least one person.

tuesday • John 5:39-47

DIGGING DEEPER · Have you ever thought you were doing something the right way, only to find out later that you weren't? It could be embarrassing, but it's usually not life-threatening. However, in the case of these religious leaders, it threatened their eternal destiny. They thought themselves to be experts in the Scripture, especially the Law of Moses (the first five books of the Old Testament). They thought that by strictly observing the law (as it was handed down and added to) they were assured of salvation. Can you imagine their shock when Jesus stated that Moses wrote of Him and the religious leaders didn't realize what He was talking about?
Do you have a relationship with the Ruler or are you strictly obeying a set of rules? The difference is relationship and where you will spend eternity.

wednesday • John 6:1-14

DIGGING DEEPER · John shares some interesting details about this miracle that aren't found in the other Gospels. First, the nearness of the Passover gives us an idea of when this miracle occurred. The testing of Philip is the second detail. Third, the bread was barley, which was coarse, cheap bread. Fourth, Andrew brings someone else to Jesus. Everyone got all they wanted to eat and Jesus asked for all the scraps to be gathered. It's interesting that there were twelve baskets and twelve disciples. Do you think this was a lesson to His disciples on God's abundant supply? There are a number of other things we can consider, like the wording found in verse 12 compared with: John 3:16; 6:39; 10:28; 18:9. Check them out.
Write down one thing you learned today? How will it change your life? Share it with someone.

thursday • John 6:15-27

DIGGING DEEPER · What happens when someone claims to have seen a miracle? People flock to see and be a part of it, too. That's what happened here. Thousands of people got a free meal and hoped they could get another. That wasn't Jesus' purpose in doing it. The miracles Jesus performed were to show His deity (that He was the Son of God) but people focused only on their physical needs and not their spiritual needs. Jesus went to the mountain to pray. Then he came to the disciples by walking on the water. This act demonstrated His power over creation and His ability to surpass the physical limitations that bind mankind.
What is your motivation in following God? What miracles (changes in lives) have you seen Jesus do lately? Share them with someone who needs encouragement.

friday • John 6:28-40

DIGGING DEEPER · When we were little children, it was important to learn how to please our parents. Likewise, the people around Jesus wanted to know what they should do to please God. *Believe in Him* is the simple answer, but the people weren't content with that. They wanted another sign like Moses feeding the people manna for forty years or some other sign that He was the Messiah. Jesus replied with the first of seven *"I AM"* statements claiming the name that God used to make Himself known to His chosen people (Exodus 3). Here He states that He is the *bread of life*. This referred to His latest miracle of feeding the five thousand and the conversation about Moses supplying bread (manna) in the wilderness.

What can you do today to please God? Is Jesus your *Bread of Life*?

saturday • John 6:41-58

DIGGING DEEPER · Have you ever been in a conversation where you were talking about one thing, but realized the other person was talking about something else? You were using the same words only they meant something different to each of you. The people wanted Jesus to throw off the oppression of Rome and meet their physical needs. They were not interested in His spiritual program. In the Gospels, Jesus spoke in parables, which often confused His casual followers. Therefore, when He presented Himself as the Bread of Life, which brings eternal life, they took it literally instead of spiritually. This passage speaks of spiritually consuming Him, the Bread of Life, by believing in Him as the Son of God.

What must you do to satisfy your soul's need for the Bread of Life? Do you seek to be fed from His Word each day?

Do people know you are a disciple of Jesus Christ because of your love for others and because you have continued in His Word? This week we'll see confused people trying to figure out just who this Jesus is. Jesus teaches spiritual truth to those who listen closely and simply believe. Will you?

Week 26

prayer focus for this week

sunday • John 6:59-71

Q

A

DIGGING DEEPER · Are you going to follow Jesus when things get rough? John points out two important truths in this passage. First, that Jesus knew from the *beginning*. This statement uses the same Greek word found in John 1:1 (the Word was with God in the *beginning*). This statement shows His foreknowledge, a characteristic that applies only to God. Secondly, verses 66 and 70 make it clear that just *following* Jesus does not guarantee that a person is a true believer. Many followers left Him. We will see later that Judas was a close follower but not a true believer in the Lord Jesus.

Are you a true follower of the Lord Jesus Christ with a living and growing faith? Attempt to do one thing today to help your faith grow (study, memorize, or witness).

monday • John 7:1-13

Q

A

DIGGING DEEPER • Do you think it would have been easier to believe in Jesus if we were alive when He walked on the earth? Most of us would not have believed. We have something they did not have—God's complete Word. Many of Jesus' followers left because they weren't true believers. Today we see that His own brothers did not believe in Him yet, and it was only six months before He would face the cross. The climate in Jerusalem was unpredictable. The people did not know who to believe. The rulers of the Jews were seeking to kill Him. Still Jesus went up secretly to be part of the Feast of Tabernacles—a celebration where the Jews were reminded of God's provision while in the wilderness. **Have you accepted God's provision of salvation? List the advantages we, as believers, have today and thank Jesus for them.**

tuesday • John 7:14-24

Q

A

DIGGING DEEPER • Have you ever had a favorite teacher? You know, one who could make the subject really come alive? Jesus was that kind of teacher. We see here that the people were amazed when they heard Him. He claimed His wisdom was from the Father above. God wants us to simply believe His Word by faith. Jesus tells of the miracle He did on the Sabbath—making a man whole. He compares it to the Law of Moses that allowed circumcision on the Sabbath. The Jews had changed their worship of God to following a set of legal rules to the letter, but God is always looking for obedience based on a relationship with Him. **How is your relationship with the Master Teacher? What is the basis of your faith? Write it out and share it with someone.**

wednesday • John 7:25-39

DIGGING DEEPER • Don't you just love holidays? Families get together and prepare special meals and activities that are only done during that time. The Feast of Tabernacles was about remembering and celebrating God's provision during forty years in the wilderness after the Exodus. One important part of the feast was a procession of people from the Pool of Siloam to the Temple. Every day the High Priest led the procession carrying a silver pitcher of water that he'd pour out into the pool. With this backdrop, Jesus proclaims that He was the source of true satisfaction and that those who find it would become a source of refreshment to others, referring to the work of the Holy Spirit that would come. **Do you need refreshing? Come to the Source of refreshment. Are you refreshing others?**

thursday • John 7:40-53

DIGGING DEEPER • Did you know that your words reveal the attitude of your heart? They reveal what you are really like on the inside. The people in the early verses show their impulsiveness. They have a range of opinions about Jesus; some call Him the *Prophet*, others the *Christ*, and yet another group claims He couldn't be either. The Pharisees, on the other hand, blasted the people for their ignorance because, they claimed none of the rulers or Pharisees believed in Him. All their lack of belief proved was that they lacked true knowledge about the Messiah in their hard hearts. Here we also see Nicodemus defending Jesus' right to a fair hearing before his peers and colleagues. **What are your words telling others about the condition of your heart? Is there an area that needs some attention? Deal with it.**

friday • John 8:1-11

DIGGING DEEPER • Have you ever been caught red-handed doing something wrong? This woman found herself in that situation. The Pharisees were trying to trap Jesus and discredit His teachings. They hoped to accuse Him of either contradicting Moses or breaking the Roman law, which didn't allow the Jews to inflict capital punishment. Jesus knew what they were up to and avoided the trap by asking them a question that exposed their motives. Notice, Jesus does not condone the woman's sin but releases her with the admonition to cease her life of immorality. She repented and was forgiven but was expected to forsake her sin.

What sin do you need to repent of and forsake today? Ask God to show you an area on which you need to work.

saturday • John 8:12-24

DIGGING DEEPER • The Pharisees were intelligent, educated men, yet they argued intensely with the Lord thinking they could change Him with their reasoning. Surely, they felt the power and meaning of His words when He said, "I am the light ...." Jesus was in the treasury of the Temple. Large lamps like hanging bonfires lit the room. Jesus made the comparison to the spiritual illumination He wanted to be in each human heart. Jesus' testimony was valid because He knew the answers to the big questions of life—*Who Am I? Where did I come from? Where am I going?*

Do you know the answers to the big questions of life? Do you know the One who already knows the answers? Ask God to reveal these to you.

Who do you think you are? That question is asked in different forms this week as we continue to follow Jesus' life. Jesus continues to deal with the growing contempt of the Pharisees as well as the controversy that came after He healed a man who was born blind. Never a dull moment... so expect some excitement.

prayer focus for this week

the Question
the Answer

What is the writer saying?

How can I apply this to my life?

sunday • John 8:25-36

Q
A

DIGGING DEEPER • Have you ever been frustrated telling a story because someone just didn't seem to understand what you were saying? That's a little of what Jesus is experiencing here. He is frustrated with the Pharisees' disrespect, and rightly so since He was clearly the Messiah with signs to verify His claims. Jesus also predicts His own death and gives specifics so that after it happens, people would remember His prediction, know that He was telling the truth, and believe. In verses 31-32, Jesus revisits two themes from the beginning of the book: the Word of God, and the Truth.

Who do you believe Jesus is? If He is your Messiah and Savior, share what He is doing in your life with someone today.

monday • John 8:37-47

DIGGING DEEPER • Things were getting a little heated between Jesus and the Pharisees, especially when Jesus pointed out who their true father was. John uses the term *your father* three times. First, it's true. They were of Abraham's physical seed, but obviously not the spiritual seed. Then, the Jews claimed God as their father, but Jesus tells them that if they loved the Father they would also love the Son, which they clearly didn't. Lastly, Jesus tells them they are sons of the devil, the father of lies, for they were doing his work. This statement was not very well received. Jesus proved His claim of speaking truth on the premise that no one could charge Him with any sin.
Who is your Father? What one thing can you do today to show (prove to) someone else who your Father is?

tuesday • John 8:48-59

DIGGING DEEPER • Have you ever been so frustrated with someone that you asked, "Just who do you think you are?" Jesus tells these *sons of Abraham* that they didn't *know* by experience the heavenly Father like He inherently *knew* Him. We can almost feel the indignation from the crowd growing. Jesus understands where they are coming from but makes it clear He is not attempting to glorify Himself, but simply carrying out His Father's will. By the end of the debate, the people were ready to stone Him to death, especially after His clearest declaration of deity when He made the *I Am* (Jehovah) claim in verse 58!
Who do you think you are? Plan how you will respond the next time someone challenges your claim of a relationship with the Lord Jesus.

wednesday • John 9:1-12

DIGGING DEEPER · Have you ever felt like you or someone close to you was being punished for some unknown sin when they seemed to suffer unjustly? Jesus makes it clear that the only reason this man was born blind was to bring glory to the Father. The man had to display his faith in Jesus by obeying what he was told to do. Throughout his Gospel, John highlights specific miracles (signs) to show that Jesus is God and bring us to the point of believing in Him. Now, He clearly illustrates this truth by bringing one born in both physical and spiritual darkness into the light.
Does your life glorify the Father? Do you believe that Jesus is God? What is Jesus asking you to do to display your faith so others can see the light?

thursday • John 9:13-25

DIGGING DEEPER · These verses show the tragedy of following man's tradition rather than walking with God. Clearly, a miracle had happened; no one disputed that. However, the religious Jews were so spiritually blind that they could look right past an incredible miracle and only see a technical violation of their Sabbath tradition. It's interesting to watch the progression of the blind man's opinion of Jesus grow from a *man* (v. 11) to a *prophet* (v. 17) to *Lord, I believe* later in verse 38. It's not the decision of parents, but rather the decision of the one who was given sight. It's a personal decision. God has no grandchildren, only sons and daughters… those who have placed their faith and trust in Him.
What best describes your spiritual walk? Is it *religion or relationship*?
Meditate on who Jesus is to you. Is He just a *man*, a *prophet*, or *your Lord*?

friday • John 9:26-41

DIGGING DEEPER • Have you ever been around small kids and learned something profound from them? It is often the simple who instruct those who claim to be educated. The man clings to the truth that he was blind but now sees, and knows that it could only be by God's awesome power. He cannot help but believe in the One who gave him this great gift. The Jews called Jesus a *sinner* because they placed their Sabbath rules above the spirit of the law. When the man was *cast out* they kicked him out of the synagogue (the local assembly of the Jews). Jesus cares for, finds the man, and reveals His deity to him. **What are you *believing* God for? Share with someone who is spiritually blind the One who can make him see.**

saturday • John 10:1-13

DIGGING DEEPER • *Just do what you believe in your heart and you'll get to heaven,* or *if your good deeds outweigh your bad, you'll get into heaven.* What is wrong with these statements? They are from the father of lies and are not true. Jesus makes His third and fourth *I Am* statements here. First, He is the Gate. In those times, the shepherd would lay down at night at the entrance of the stone corral to protect his sheep. He literally became the door. The message is exclusive… *there is only one way!* (v. 7; John 14:6; 1 Timothy 2:5). Secondly, Jesus is the Good Shepherd. You've heard it all your life, but what does it really mean? To find out compare the following verses: Zechariah 11:4-9, Psalm 22, Hebrews 13:20, Psalm 23, 1 Peter 5:4, and Psalm 24. **Is Jesus your Gate to Heaven and your Shepherd? Prove it by your actions!**

Is Jesus your Good Shepherd? This would be a good week to decide. This week we'll see Jesus proclaiming His relationship with the Father, which enrages the Pharisees who will seek to kill Him. We will also see several instances that show Jesus knows what's happening in other places as well as in the future.

prayer focus for this week

the Question
the Answer

What is the writer saying?

How Can I apply this to my life?

sunday • John 10:14-30

Q
A

DIGGING DEEPER • Is Jesus your Good Shepherd? John explains the special relationship Jesus has with His sheep. It is the *knowing* that is important. The Father loves the Son and Jesus was totally willing to obey, even if it meant facing the cross. Verses 17 and 18 clearly teach that Jesus was in total control throughout the events leading up to His crucifixion. He willingly laid down His life as a sacrifice for each one of us. Jesus was speaking during the Feast of Dedication (today's Jewish celebration of Hanukkah in December). This passage concludes (vv. 27-30) with a powerful declaration of the security all believers can have in their eternal future.

How secure are you in *knowing* Jesus as your Good Shepherd? Are you willing to obey anything the Father asks you to do? Think about it!

monday • John 10:31-42

Q
A

DIGGING DEEPER • Have you ever been upset by something someone else said? The Jews understood perfectly Jesus' statement in verse 30, that He and the Father are one. They lashed out calling it blasphemy. Jesus quoted Psalm 82:6 where the Psalmist used the common Hebrew word for God, *Elohim*. He also let His works speak for Him. Again, we see that Jesus was in complete control of the situation as He eluded their grasp when they wanted to stone Him. His ministry returns to where it began—a place beyond the Jordan where John first baptized. There were many who sought Him and would believe in Him there. Being at the right place at the right time allows you to bear fruit for the Lord. **Will you stand for God when challenged by the world? What do your works say to those around you about your relationship with Jesus?**

tuesday • John 11:1-15

DIGGING DEEPER • Do you know what goes on at your friend's house when you're at home, or what's going to happen tomorrow? Of course not! It's amazing to observe in this passage that Jesus, being God, not only knew what was going on at His friend's house (which was around 20 miles away!), but also what was going to happen four days ahead of time. He explained to His disciples that this episode was going to glorify both God the Father and God the Son. This final sign (miracle) before the crucifixion points to the newness of life that awaits those who have trusted Christ as Savior. **Do you trust God to know about and be in control of what's going on in your life, both today and in the future? Write two things for which you are trusting Him.**

wednesday • John 11:16-29

DIGGING DEEPER • To lose someone close to you is a very painful thing and everyone handles it in his own individual way. Martha ran to the Lord as soon as she heard He was coming and discussed the resurrection with Him. Mary waited and mourned until she was told that Jesus was near and wanted to see her. Here is something interesting to think about—the Jews of that day believed the soul of a person did not leave for Heaven until three days had passed. Notice that Jesus purposely waited until the fourth day to increase the drama and impact of this crowning sign (miracle), the restoring of Lazarus from the dead. Wouldn't it have been neat to witness this? Even if we didn't see it, we can believe it as God recorded it for us. **Thank God for dealing with each of us as individuals. Ask Him to help you meet people where they are.**

thursday • John 11:30-44

DIGGING DEEPER • Have you ever been surprised when something bigger and better happened than what you expected? Maybe it was for a birthday or Christmas. When Mary reached Jesus, she used words that were almost identical to the ones Martha had used. She showed a firm conviction that they believed Jesus could have saved Lazarus from death. Jesus exceeded all that they thought could have happened! Many Christians are like Lazarus when he came out of the tomb—alive in Christ, but still bound by the grave clothes of the world. They cannot work or witness because their hands and mouths are bound. **If you are a Christian, are you totally free from the *bondage* of this world? Ask Jesus to reveal any area that binds you and ask Him to help you work on releasing it.**

friday • John 11:45-57

DIGGING DEEPER • What would you have done if you were in the crowd that witnessed Lazarus coming out of the tomb? Of course, you would believe, right? However, we see that some simply went to report the incident to the authorities. Their hearts were hardened to the truth. When the Pharisees discussed this new miracle, they openly plotted to kill Jesus (which Jesus predicted in John 8:44). The Passover was at hand. Jesus would soon be the ultimate Passover Lamb. His blood would be a once-for-all sacrifice that would serve not as a covering for sin (which Passover represented), but as the satisfaction of God's righteous demands (1 John 2:2). It was to be the cleansing from sin for those who believe (Hebrews 10:10-14).
Share this story with someone today and ask what he would have done.

saturday • John 12:1-11

DIGGING DEEPER • Sometimes it's hard to distinguish time in the Bible. It would seem that the events in today's text happened shortly after Lazarus was raised from the dead, but about three months has passed. Martha was still serving while Mary was worshipping. The value of the perfume is overwhelming because it was rare, being from India. Would you spend a year's wages on something and then pour it on someone's feet? No one suspected Judas of thievery at the time. Mary, Martha, and Lazarus are wonderful examples of service, fellowship, and worship. Judas and the Pharisees are examples of greed and sinful intents of the heart. Many lives, many needs… but one Redeemer.
With which group do you line up? What are you willing to place at Jesus' feet?

Did you know that what you believe about Jesus is the key to your future, and blessing is found in doing what pleases God? This week we'll see Jesus pleasing God from the time He entered Jerusalem with people who hoped He was the Messiah, to quietly humbling Himself as He washed the disciples' feet.

Week 29

the Question
the Answer

What is the writer saying?

How Can I apply this to my life?

sunday • John 12:12-22

Q

A

DIGGING DEEPER · Wouldn't you like to have been in the crowd that day? This is one of the few events recorded in all four Gospels so it must be significant. There is Old Testament symbolism here that could be easy to miss. For example, the palm branch was a symbol of happiness. Hosanna means *please save*. Both this phrase and *He who comes* are found in Psalm 118:25-26. The crowd obviously had these messianic ideas in mind as they greeted Jesus. His entry, riding on a donkey's colt, is a fulfillment of Zechariah 9:9. Again, the disciples didn't fully understand what happened here until after Christ's resurrection.

Read the above Scriptures to see how Jesus fulfilled them. All things written about Jesus will be fulfilled. Are you ready for His return?

monday • John 12:23-36

DIGGING DEEPER • Did you notice that no more mention is made of the Gentiles' request? However, Jesus uses this as an opportunity to predict His pending death. Verse 25 is a paradox. Those who wish to save their life (living for their own selfish ends) will destroy that to which they desperately cling. Those who hate their lives (by selflessly living to glorify God) gain true life indeed. John returns to the familiar theme of light versus darkness and the faith that leads to belief. The more light we have, the more accountable we are. For many of us, the problem is not that we don't know what to do, but living up to what we already know is true.

What are you doing with what you know about Jesus? Praise God for giving you the opportunity to enjoy special benefits as His child.

tuesday • John 12:37-50

DIGGING DEEPER • Are you asking, "How could those who witnessed these miracles not believe?" It is hard for us who have the whole Bible to understand their hard hearts. Some who reject the deity of Christ say Scripture does not refer to Jesus by the name *Jehovah*. However, there is a direct connection in verse 41 that refers to Isaiah 6:1 where John tells us that the prophet beheld the glory of Jesus. Those who reject Jesus Christ only have themselves to blame. Jesus makes it clear that those who hear and reject the Gospel will be judged by the very Word of God from which they have turned away.

How are you responding to the truth of the Gospel? Thank the person(s) who took the time to share it with you. With whom do you need to share it?

wednesday • John 13:1-11

DIGGING DEEPER • What would you think if the President of the United States came to dinner at your house and washed everyone's feet? Someone far more important washed the disciples' feet! Jesus showed His disciples how much He loved them by leaving them an example of humility to follow. This was done only one day before Jesus would be crucified. In the exchange between Peter and Jesus, more than dirty feet was discussed. Jesus' reply in verse 10 is a reference to salvation. "He that is washed," (saved) "needs only to wash his feet" (confession of daily sins). Believers are bathed in the blood of Jesus Christ for salvation and kept in fellowship by the confession of daily sin. **Who do you need to humble yourself before today? Let Jesus wash you spiritually by confessing your sin to Him and asking His forgiveness.**

thursday • John 13:12-20

DIGGING DEEPER • Did you know that washing feet was usually the task of the lowest servant of the house? Jesus showed that as their Teacher and Lord, He was not too good to serve them. They were not too good to serve one another either. If our Lord was humble enough to wash the disciples' feet, who are we to consider ourselves above serving others, no matter how lowly the job? Blessing is not found in the knowledge of what is pleasing to God, but in *doing* those things that please Him. Jesus also plainly tells them of His betrayal before it occurred, so that after it happened, their faith would not be shaken, but strengthened. **Be like Christ and serve someone unexpectedly today. *Do* something that you know will please God (memory work, witnessing, or caring).**

friday • John 13:21-38

DIGGING DEEPER • It's hard to be around someone you know is going to die. Jesus tells His disciples to brace themselves because He's going to be leaving them. They don't totally understand. Peter privately tells John to ask Jesus who the betrayer is. He asks and gets the correct answer when Jesus plainly identifies Judas. However, the other disciples were oblivious to what was going on. When Jesus tells them that they can't follow Him, He softens the statement by indicating that their separation would be temporary, not permanent. Jesus calls Peter on his intent to lay down his life for Him by stating the reality to come.

Will you be able to follow Jesus like Peter in verse 37? Are you willing to lay down your life for Jesus? He knows the reality to come!

saturday • John 14:1-14

DIGGING DEEPER • The sixth of Christ's great *I Am* statements is found in verse 6. Jesus, being one with the Father, was of the same fundamental nature as the Father. To know Jesus was equal to knowing the Father. Belief is the key. Those who know Jesus know the way home! The astounding statement that the disciples would do *greater works* is understood as greater in scope. Jesus, who limited Himself by taking on an earthly body, was ministering in a specific geographical area. Now with the Holy Spirit living in believers, we have the privilege of seeing lives changed through the power of the Gospel all over the world at the same time.

Do you believe Jesus and the Father are one? Act on it, and share who Jesus is with someone needing Good News today.

Have you ever been confused about the ministry of the Holy Spirit? Many ask, "Where does He fit in with God the Father and God the Son?" Jesus will reveal this week how the Holy Spirit convicts us of sin, encourages to righteousness, and helped the disciples write the New Testament.

Week 30

prayer focus for this week

the Question
the Answer

What is the writer saying?

How Can I apply this to my life?

sunday • John 14:15-24

Q

A

DIGGING DEEPER • Do you love God? You can prove it by obeying God's Word and following Jesus' example. Verses 15 and 24 are like the bookends of this section. Obedience to the commandments of God characterizes the life of the true believer. Jesus set the ultimate example of love and obedience. Now He expects His followers to walk according to that same pattern. The other Comforter that Jesus used here is the Greek word allos, which means another of the same kind. Both Jesus and the Holy Spirit are of the same kind and should comfort us.

Again, do you love God? Do the people around you see your obedience to God's commands? Think of one thing that you know God commands you to do in His Word and do it.

monday • John 14:25-31

DIGGING DEEPER • Do you remember what your friends have said to you over the last three years? Jesus tells His disciples that one of the ministries of the Holy Spirit would be to help them remember all He had said, even when they didn't understand it at the time. The ministry of the Holy Spirit is different after the cross than before it. The actual payment for the sin of mankind gave the Spirit of God greater influence in the lives of men than the Old Testament saints experienced. Notice that it was with unwavering obedience and submission to the will of the Heavenly Father that Jesus Christ walked full face into the adversary's fury.
What is the Holy Spirit helping you remember from God's Word? Is there something specific He's asking you to obey? Will you do it?

tuesday • John 15:1-11

DIGGING DEEPER • As Jesus and the disciples left the Last Supper and went to the Garden of Gethsemane they passed olive gardens. Jesus used this as an analogy to describe the relationship He had with believers. The result is increasing fruitfulness. The gardener prunes the branches that are in the vine to maximize their fruit bearing. Verse 7 is not a blank check but a promise that His disciples could rely on Christ to meet their needs as they walked in obedience. This relationship that Jesus describes for His disciples was based on love and obedience, just as His relationship with His Father. Their walk of love and obedience would result in glory to the Father and fullness of joy for them.
Are you walking in love and obedience? Are you being pruned?

wednesday • John 15:12-27

DIGGING DEEPER • In yesterday's passage, we see Jesus talking to the disciples about their relationship with Him. Today He talks to them about their relationship with each other. In that day, students chose the rabbi they wanted to study under. Jesus says He reversed the process by choosing them. He chose them to be fruit bearers. Jesus warns them that the world is not going to treat them kindly. The last two verses return to the coming of the Comforter who will energize them in their relationship. They will be as a light, a witness, and a testimony to the world. Notice that the Holy Spirit's job is to magnify Christ, not Himself.

We are free to choose to show our gratitude to our Savior by working for Him and His glory. What can you do today to show your gratitude to Christ?

thursday • John 16:1-11

DIGGING DEEPER • Have you ever been confused about the role of the Holy Spirit? Jesus explains what the Spirit's role will be. There are three areas stated in verse 8 and explained in verses 9-11. First, the Spirit is to bring conviction of sin to the world. Second, the Spirit convicts of righteousness and sin among Jesus' followers. Third, the Spirit will warn of coming judgment. Jesus warns them to expect to be outcasts so they would not be caught off guard when it happened. Being put out of the synagogue was serious. Birth certificates, marriage certificates, divorce, and burial rights were all controlled by the synagogue and the Pharisees.

Is the Holy Spirit convicting you of an area of righteousness that you need to work on? Judgment is coming! Are you ready?

friday • John 16:12-22

DIGGING DEEPER • Another part of the ministry of the Holy Spirit is teaching. Jesus pre-authenticates the whole of the New Testament writings to come. "Bring all things to your remembrance" (14:26) speaks of the Gospels. "Guide you into all truth" refers to the Epistles being penned under the Holy Spirit's inspiration. These letters would give the early Church (and us) much needed direction and instruction. "Show you things to come" was the promise of the blessing of the completed Bible. The book of Revelation would foretell the final chapter of human history and the glorious future for those who are born again and thus will enter into God's rest.
What is the Spirit teaching you today? Let Him guide you in understanding God's revealed Word.

saturday • John 16:23-33

DIGGING DEEPER • When was the last time you didn't pray *in Jesus' name*? Reference is made in verse 23 to a time after Jesus' resurrection when He would give us a pattern to follow. They were to pray to the Father in the authority of the Son and empowered by the Holy Spirit. It is hard to think that anything could be better than having Jesus living with you in the flesh. However, in the plan of God, the indwelling Holy Spirit and His written Word gives us a richer relationship with the Godhead. Jesus leaves us with an example to follow in our lonely times as He rightly points out that the Father would be with Him when He knew the disciples would flee.
Consciously think about each person of the Godhead as you pray using the above pattern. Thank Jesus for what you know is going to come.

Have you ever dreaded an upcoming week? Perhaps you faced mid-terms or finals you knew would be stressful. This week, we'll see Jews trying to kill Jesus, Gentiles trying to free him, and others venting their frustrations on Him. With all this going on, Jesus stays focused on the job He came to do.

Week 31

prayer focus for this week

the Question
the Answer

What is the writer saying?

How Can I apply this to my life?

sunday • John 17:1-13

Q

A

DIGGING DEEPER • Would you like the Lord Himself to pray specifically for you? He does here. This is Jesus' high-priestly prayer of intercession. Verses 1-5 are a prayer between Father and Son. Jesus asks the Father to "glorify thy Son," meaning His authority, and to "glorify thou me," meaning His return to His pre-incarnate glory. Second, the prayer broadened to include the disciples. There are two prayers in verses 6-19 to "keep them" (from evil) and "sanctify them" (set them apart for His work). Then verses 20-26 contain two requests: I ask for unity among all believers, and I desire to unite all believers with their Savior in glory. **Are you part of all believers? Thank Him for praying for you! Are you living in unity with others and working together to do things that glorify Jesus?**

monday • John 17:14-26

DIGGING DEEPER • Isn't it comforting to know that Jesus was looking down through history at us as He prayed? We are not of this world as shown in verse 8. First, we accept His Words. Second, we recognize that Jesus came from the Father. Third, we believe Him. Note the close association in verse 17 between sanctification (to be set apart for God's use) and revealed truth. Those 11 disciples began a long chain of unity and hard work that reaches down the corridors of time to us in the twenty-first century. Hopefully the result was your salvation! We are to take the disciples as our example. We are to be set apart and continue where they left off.

Are you a promoter of unity, or are you a weak link by sowing discord in your local church? Thank those who shared Jesus with you!

tuesday • John 18:1-14

DIGGING DEEPER • The Cedron (Kidron) was a steep valley between Jerusalem and the Mount of Olives. The band (cohort) of men that Judas brought numbered 300-600 soldiers! Christ responds with the name of Jehovah, "I Am." The response of the soldiers shows that they knew what He said. This display of power is a reminder that Jesus did not have His life taken from Him but laid it down willingly. Peter tries to take charge of the situation. He does not realize that the events are part of God's plan. Jesus stops him and announces His intentions to go with the men. He is taken to Annas who was the real power behind the High Priest.

Are you studying God's Word so that you will know truth from error? Are you fulfilling God's plan or trying to take charge yourself?

wednesday • John 18:15-27

DIGGING DEEPER • What would you have done if you had witnessed the events that night? Only two of the disciples followed Jesus... and it was at a distance. These two were Peter and John and their names are not given, perhaps out of humility. The high priest's questions were focused on two areas: Jesus' disciples and His teaching. He was more concerned with who followed Jesus than what Jesus taught. Interwoven with Jesus' questioning is the drama of Peter's three denials. When comparing the four Gospel accounts, some have been confused about the identity of the questioners. Many people around the fire could have questioned Peter. Each author reports the questioner who caught his attention in the retelling of the events of that fateful night. **What kind of witness are you? When under fire, will you leave or follow?**

thursday • John 18:28-40

DIGGING DEEPER • Do your actions ever contradict what is going on in your heart? Look at how the Jews didn't want to go into the Praetorium (hall of judgment). They didn't want to defile themselves while they were in the process of planning a murder! Jesus answers Pilate clearly stating that He is a King, but not of this world. Note that Pilate does not probe the answer, but simply concludes that Jesus is indeed claiming to be a king. What he does next by asking "what is truth" seems to show an indifference to Jesus' words. Pilate appears to neither believe Him nor find Him to be a threat, but looks for a way to set Him free. **How are your actions portraying what is going on in your heart? Do those around you know of your belief in Jesus?**

friday • John 19:1-11

Q

A

DIGGING DEEPER · Have you gotten confused about the charges against Jesus? The original charge against Him before Pilate was treason (John 18:33).The Sanhedrin thought charging Him with treason would be easier than explaining the real charge of blasphemy. Pilate wasn't willing to execute an innocent man so he beat Jesus to try to satisfy the Sanhedrin. Perhaps Pilate thought to arouse pity to release Jesus. He also allowed his soldiers to take their frustrations out on the Jews by mocking their king. Jesus maintains a dignified silence fulfilling Isaiah 53:7. Jesus minimizes Pilate's role in the crucifixion by placing the blame on the Jews.
These are not the best choices, but whose place would you select? The Jews who wanted Jesus killed, Pilate who tried to release Him, or the soldiers who took their frustrations out on an innocent man?

saturday • John 19:12-22

Q

A

DIGGING DEEPER · Have you ever tried to trick someone into saying something? Pilate baits the Jews into professing heresy when they say, "We have no king but Caesar." After this, he realized the hardness of their hearts and turned Jesus over to be crucified. The purpose of Roman crucifixion was two-fold. First, the agony of the event was designed to discourage rebellion. The other was total humiliation. The condemned had to endure the cruelty of carrying his own instrument of death while suffering the shame of public nakedness. It is natural to concentrate on the physical horror of crucifixion, but also keep in mind the spiritual results of the humiliation, selfless love, sin bearing, and the spiritual death.
Think deeply about what Jesus did when He willingly was crucified for you.

This week is going to be exciting as we examine fulfilled prophecy, confusion about the resurrection, and Jesus' appearances after the crucifixion. John declares himself an eyewitness to all the things concerning Jesus' ministry. He wants the result of reading this book to be belief in Jesus. Do you believe?

Week 32

prayer focus for this week

theQuestion
theAnswer

What is the writer saying?

How Can I apply this to my life?

sunday • John 19:23-30

Q

A

DIGGING DEEPER · Have you ever tried to write a mystery story where all the clues needed to be given, but in such a way that the outcome was not obvious? It's a difficult thing. We see evidence of God's sovereignty in the fulfillment of prophecy (Psalm 22:18, 69:21) – even down to how they would treat him. Jesus' concern for His mother is touching. Woman was not a disrespectful way to address one's mother in that culture. "Behold thy son" was instructive to Mary as He commends her to John's care. The care of a widow was the responsibility of the oldest son. Jesus entrusts His mother to the care of John rather than His unbelieving brothers. Jesus' love and concern was evident to the end!

To whom can you show love and concern for today in Jesus' name?

monday · John 19:31-42

DIGGING DEEPER · Are you familiar enough with the Old Testament prophecies to know which were actually fulfilled in Jesus' first coming? Here John tells us of two more: Exodus 12:46 and Zechariah 12:10. This particular Sabbath was a high day. It was the first day of the Feast of Unleavened Bread that year. John injects some strong emotion (vv. 35-37) identifying himself as an eyewitness to Christ's death explaining what he saw. Water is the plasma that separates from the red blood cells after the heart stops. Two influential men secure the body, allowing it to suffer no more indignity.
Look up the Old Testament passages listed the last few days and be a witness to someone of all that God fulfilled through Jesus.

tuesday · John 20:1-10

DIGGING DEEPER · The ironic tragedy of the life of Jesus is resolved in the resurrection. "Although virtuous, He suffered all possible indignities; majestic, he died in disgrace; powerful, he expired in weakness. He claimed to possess the water of life but died thirsty; to be the light of the world, but died in darkness; to be the Good Shepherd, but died in the fangs of wolves; to be the Truth, but was executed as an imposter; to be Life itself, but He died quicker than the average crucifixion victim. The greatest example of righteousness the world had ever seen became a helpless victim of evil!" (Merrill Tenney)
Think through the above statements carefully and thank Jesus for what He did for you. Share this with someone who needs hope today.

wednesday • John 20:11-18

DIGGING DEEPER • What would you have believed if you were there that morning? We see the confusion of those closest to Him. Mary was sobbing broken-heartedly when she looks in the tomb. She sees the angels and talks to them but nothing is registering. She turns and notices another man and launches into a fresh attempt to locate the body of her Lord. Finally, through her tears, she hears the familiar voice and realizes she is talking to her Lord! Two natural acts follow. First, she uses the familiar name Master and then clings to Jesus with a grip that hinted she would never let go. Jesus didn't want Mary to cling to Him. She needed to go and tell others and then learn to trust Him by relying on the soon coming Holy Spirit.

Mary was forgiven much and loved much. How much do you love Jesus?

thursday • John 20:19-31

DIGGING DEEPER • Wouldn't you like to have been one of the first to see the resurrected Lord? We don't know how many were gathered there that night, perhaps as many as eleven. We do know they were afraid. Imagine how they must have been dissecting every detail that Mary, Peter, and John provided. Suddenly, Jesus was there. They were fearful of His sudden appearance and their actions earlier. Jesus spoke to them with a routine greeting of peace to calm their fears. Before we're too hard on Thomas, remember that the very proof he requested had already been provided for those who were there. The purpose of the book of John is clearly stated in verse 31, "… that ye might have life through His name."

Do you believe? Don't be afraid to share the Gospel with someone who doubts what the world has to offer. We know Jesus is the answer!

friday • John 21:1-14

DIGGING DEEPER • Having established belief in the life and message of Jesus Christ, John now tells us how this message spreads throughout the world. Jesus appeared to the disciples on their familiar home ground. This cancelled out any sense that what they experienced in Jerusalem was a product of their fear and confusion. Christ appears to men who should have recognized Him, but they didn't. Jesus, being God, knew they hadn't caught any fish and tells them where to cast the net. They obey and realize it is the Lord as they remembered three years earlier when Jesus first called them to ministry. **Write down some things Jesus has done for you since you were saved. Thank Him for providing them for you. Now share that with someone.**

saturday • John 21:15-25

DIGGING DEEPER • Have you ever wanted to take back something that you said in frustration? Peter had publicly denied the Lord three times after professing a greater love than others. Now, Christ gives Peter three chances to affirm his love for Him publicly. The Master Shepherd mentions two aspects of shepherding – feeding and caring for all their needs. John closes his Gospel declaring that his life served as an eyewitness account of the greatest Man who ever lived. It was his desire for those who read his account to believe in the Lord Jesus Christ as their personal Savior. **Do you believe? Are you willing to follow Jesus wherever He leads and do what He asks? Would those around you affirm that you are a Christian?**

Are you ready for some wisdom? As usual, Proverbs will provide some great insight in the areas of wisdom, instruction, and knowledge. As you open your Bible this week, open up your mind to wisdom as well. Wisdom is knowledge (information) used properly.

Week 33

prayer focus for this week

the Question
the Answer

What is the writer saying?

How Can I apply this to my life?

sunday • Proverbs 16:1-11

Q
A

DIGGING DEEPER • Most people like to be in control. They want to pick the vacation destination, the restaurant Sunday after church, and they even want to pick out their own Christmas presents. Leaders love to make the decisions. Sometimes this gets them into trouble though, especially if their relationship with God is not quite right. We want to be in control of our lives. And while our intentions may not be impure, we must make sure that we commit our plans to our Heavenly Father. Today's passage has many great truths, but verse 3 may speak loudest to us. Let God be the leader of your life. Don't try to live the Christian life in your own strength. Seek the help that He offers and commit all that you do to Him.
Do you let God lead you in life or do you feel you need to make all the decisions? How can you allow God to lead you more?

monday • Proverbs 16:12-22

DIGGING DEEPER • In life we are going to have people who supervise us. These people may be principals and teachers in school. They may be bosses at work. They are government officials and parents. God placed these people over us for a reason. They should use that position for doing what is good and right. People in these positions need to exercise or use wisdom in all their decision-making. We should respond favorably to their leadership. It may be that we will be placed in a position of leadership. When in that position, we should not be proud, but instead be humble and speak with care and understanding.

How do you treat the people that God has placed over you? What are you doing to prepare yourself to be the right kind of leader?

tuesday • Proverbs 6:23-33

DIGGING DEEPER • We live in a day when it seems okay to put people down. We usually do it with derogatory statements and snide remarks. At the time, we justify it as being right because it's funny. As we get older we look back and see how bad some of the comments were and how they, in reality, hurt someone with whom we may have been friends. God's Word says how important our words are. Look closely again at this section and note how valuable pleasant words are and the danger of unpleasant words. Then, do your best to speak as this proverb recommends. If you've been a member of the wrecking crew perhaps it's time to change and become part of the construction crew.

How do you talk to your friends? Are your words tearing them down or building them up?

wednesday • Proverbs 17:1-9

DIGGING DEEPER • Proverbs is noted for its contrasts. Today's passage is no exception as it starts off with either strife or harmony. It is better to have a little with contentment than abundance with no peace. Then it talks about deceitfulness. While some may defend being deceitful, Scripture says it is equivalent to lying, cheating, and stealing. Cheating in school is always an issue. It is just a lot easier to cheat than to actually do the work. Stealing and cheating are one and the same because you are taking what someone else has done and using it as your own. All of these: lying, stealing, and cheating, should be removed from your life, along with the sin of deceitfulness.
What are you doing today that will cause you to fail God's test? What can you change about yourself so you will pass God's test?

thursday • Proverbs 17:10-19

DIGGING DEEPER • These verses show the similarities between the foolish man and the evil man. The evil man is someone who rebels when rebuked. The foolish man is shown as a person who just doesn't change. He is someone who doesn't care about doing what is right. A popular notion today is that rebellion as a teen is just part of growing up, but the Bible says that it is characteristic of someone who is evil. As a teenager, there is also some expectation that you're going to get into trouble. Scripture again says that this is the characteristic of a fool. It's obvious that the path of both the foolish and evil man must be avoided.
Is rebelling against your parents a part of your lifestyle? If so, are you willing to change?

friday • Proverbs 17:20-28

DIGGING DEEPER • There are many nuggets of truth and good advice in all of these verses but look at verse 28. You have probably heard something similar to it. We've all heard someone stick their foot in their mouth. Did you know that even a foolish person could appear to be wise when they say nothing? Sometimes just saying nothing is the best thing you can do. The story is told of a man in California who was out of work and needed some money. He put an ad in a local paper saying: "I will listen to your problems for thirty minutes." The response was enormous. His schedule was full for at least eight hours a day most days. That man made some serious money just listening. We could learn a lesson from that man. **Do you need to listen more? Think of one person that may need you to listen to them.**

saturday • Proverbs 18:1-12

DIGGING DEEPER • The expression "The name of the Lord" is found only here in Proverbs. It stands for the many perfections of God such as faithfulness, mercy, and wisdom. The Christian relies on these things for security. As teenagers, we may be insecure in a lot of areas in our lives and lack the understanding we need to have of God. Things such as God's wisdom or mercy do not mean much to us right now, but they will. The thing we need to concern ourselves with is God's faithfulness. That will bring some security to us as we realize that God will do what He says. God is a place of security and trust and He wants you to run to Him.
Are you running to God or from God with your problems? If you are not running to God, then to whom or what are you running?

We all need practical advice and this week we'll get plenty of it. Advice on listening, laziness, and lying await you among many other marvelous truths. Check it out.

Week 34

prayer focus for this week

sunday • Proverbs 18:13-24

Q

A

DIGGING DEEPER · Do you know what it's like to have an argument with your brother or sister? Sure you do, unless you're an only child; and some of you have had some pretty good arguments with other people's brothers and sisters, too! Many of the verses in this section deal with our relationships with other people. They give us advice on how to deal with others, including our siblings. Maybe we're guilty of talking too soon, too much, too offensively, or even too harshly. After an argument with a sibling, it is often very hard to make up with them. This obviously is not good. God wants us to be broken before Him and allow Him to restore that relationship to where it should be. **Do you have a broken relationship with someone in your family? If so, has God spoken to your heart about fixing it?**

monday • Proverbs 19:1-9

DIGGING DEEPER · In these verses, a wealthy man and a poor man are mentioned several times. The Bible never speaks out against having a lot or not having much, but it does tell us about the reality of both of these circumstances. We sometimes dream about having a lot of money and the things that it could buy, the people it could introduce us to, the cars it could buy us, the house it could give us, and the ability to let us do the things we want to do in life. As we get older, all that will change. Yes, money is nice but it doesn't buy happiness. In the end, you will feel better about yourself if you are poor and have integrity and true friends than if you are rich with no integrity and no real friends.
What do you think brings true happiness? Make a short list of the most valuable things in your life.

tuesday • Proverbs 19:10-19

DIGGING DEEPER · Verse 16 is our key verse today. What it's saying is that if you keep God's wisdom, you are kept safe, and if you are careless and don't keep God's wisdom, then you step out from under the umbrella of God's protection. How many of you have parents that tell you what to do? Almost all of you, right? We've all felt the strain of being told what we should and should not do. But what we may not understand at the time is that there is an important reason why parents don't want us to do certain things. It's not because they are trying to make us miserable. No, rather it's that they see the big picture for our lives. They know the potential dangers and risks of being involved in certain activities. God is the same way. He sees the big picture and knows what is best.
How are you living today? Are you following God's commands?

wednesday • Proverbs 19:20-29

DIGGING DEEPER • In verse 20, we are instructed to listen to counsel and receive instruction, so that we can be wise later on in life. The importance of listening to God and our parents when we are younger is to make us wiser when we are older. Some have looked back at their lives as teenagers and are glad they listened to advice from wise people, including their parents. When we follow advice, things usually turn out as we expect. When we don't follow advice, things turn out as we expect, too, but for the worse. Experience is a great teacher and that's why it is important to listen to your parents and people who care about you. They don't want to see you mess up, but rather want to see you succeed.

Do you listen and put into practice the advice that is given to you?

thursday • Proverbs 20:1-10

DIGGING DEEPER • A common theme among several of our verses today is the subject of righteousness or having a right standing before God. Verse 7 tells us that a person in good standing before God should not have anything to fear about what he has done because he has integrity, even in the secret and dark places. Some have done things they are ashamed of and wouldn't want people finding out about because they are Christians. People could easily get wrong ideas about Christians. That's an indication that we are not walking in integrity. God takes no delight in our failure. Yet, in our imperfection, God is the only one who can cleanse us and make our relationship right.

Are you living life afraid of being found out? Are you spiritually pure?

friday • Proverbs 20:11-20

DIGGING DEEPER • Verse 11 tells us that every person is known by his actions. Yesterday we talked about walking in integrity and that sometimes we don't always walk the talk of the Christian. This verse goes so well with that. If you're a Christian you will be known as a Christian only by what you do and how you act. If you are not a Christian, the same is also true. You will be known by what you do and how you act. So then, there is a responsibility that every Christian must be regularly aware of. We must live the life, day in, day out, in our homes, and at our schools. Before, during, and after church, we must live the life.

Whose child are you? What are you known for? Do others know you are a Christian by the way you act?

saturday • Proverbs 20:21-30

DIGGING DEEPER • None of us likes being trampled on, talked about, or hurt in any way. God knows that. But He tells us in verse 22, to not respond to evil with evil. Don't try to get back at someone. God tells us that for our good because only He can determine the proper judgment of an individual and execute it perfectly. It is not our place to do that. When we step in and try to judge, we are trying to take the place of God. We, in a nutshell, are saying, I am God and I alone can give that person what they deserve and know what that punishment should be. That's dangerous ground to be walking on, so let's stay away from it altogether.

What kind of grudges are you holding on to? What are you planning to do with those grudges?

Do you ever wonder what God's plans are for your life? This week we get to read about how God speaks to Zechariah through eight visions in one night! As we see God's ultimate plan for Israel, we'll take some time to reflect on how each of us fit into God's plan for eternity. So, what are you waiting for?

Week 35

prayer focus for this week

the Question
the Answer

What is the writer saying?

How Can I apply this to my life?

sunday · Zechariah 1:1-6

Q

A

DIGGING DEEPER · Do you ever ignore your parent's instructions because obedience seems hard or inconvenient? We have all done this, and every one of us has been disobedient to God, as well. We choose to ignore Gods commands. This is sin, and our sin has consequences. The Jewish people had given up rebuilding the temple because they were afraid of their enemies. Rather than trust God, they feared man and stopped doing God's work. God sends Zechariah to call the people to repentance. The people agree that their actions were wrong. Repentance is the beginning of having a right relationship with God.
Has God been convicting you of some sin in your life? Take time today to confess your sins to God and take a look at these verses: Psalm 51:2-4, 1 John 1:8-10, and Romans 6:12.

monday • Zechariah 1:7-17

DIGGING DEEPER • Do you ever wonder where you fit into God's greater plan? Today's passage is about the people of Israel and their part in God's plan. After Zechariah's message on repentance, God gives him eight visions in one night. The first vision is of a rider on a red horse. The rider is The Angel of the Lord, which is a name used in the Old Testament to identify God. This vision portrays God watching over Israel. The Lord says in verse 16 that He has returned to Israel *with mercies.* The temple will soon be rebuilt. Verse 17 looks forward to the future kingdom age. God has a plan for Israel which has already begun and will not be completed until the Millennium.
If you're struggling to understand what you are going through today, remember that you are part of His eternal plan. The choices you make today matter for eternity.

tuesday • Zechariah 1:18-21

DIGGING DEEPER • Does your current situation seem difficult or scary? Do you ever wonder what God's plan is for this world? No matter what is taking place in the world around you and regardless of how you feel today, God is sovereign. He has been and always will be in control. Here, Zechariah receives his second vision from the Lord. This prophecy tells about three events that have already occurred and one that is to come. The four horns represent nations that come to scatter God's people. God used Persia to defeat Babylon, Greece to defeat Persia, and Rome to defeat Greece. The horns and the craftsmen are the same nations with the exception of the final horn, which is Jesus.
God knows the trials and tribulations you are facing. Your problems are not too big for God. So give them over to Him. He wants to take your heavy load.

wednesday • Zechariah 2:1-13

DIGGING DEEPER · Are you ever scared? Perhaps you're afraid of something and you wish you had someone to protect you. As Christians, God is our Protector. This vision is a prophecy of the Millennium. Verse 4 talks of a time when Jerusalem will be so heavily populated that there will be no walls to hold all of its inhabitants. Verse 5 talks of the Lord being their wall of protection. The Lord always watches over His people Israel. Zechariah is a message of hope for Israel's future. Israel will be scattered, but as we look to the Millennium when God's plan for Israel will be complete, we see that God will gather the nation together again. Verse 13 talks of the Millennium when the whole earth will be silent because God is in His temple. **As a child of God you are precious to Him. He wants to spend time with you. Spend some time in prayer with your Heavenly Father and just enjoy Him.**

thursday • Zechariah 3:1-10

DIGGING DEEPER · Do you ever feel like you can't stop sinning? Do you feel burdened and stained by your sin? Take heart, that's not the way God sees us. He sees us as forgiven! Joshua was the High Priest in Zechariah's day. On the Day of Atonement the High Priest would go into the Holy of Holies as a representative for the entire nation. In this vision Joshuas' filthy garments are a representation of the sin of Israel. We see Satan at his right side accusing him. But the Lord removes his iniquities and puts him in beautiful priestly garments for service, which represents God clothing Him in the righteousness of Christ. Looking at Joshua, we see not only the sin of Israel, but our sin as well. Satan is our accuser, but Jesus is our Redeemer. We were once condemned, but when we place our trust in Christ, we are redeemed. **Our righteousness is as filthy rags (Isaiah 64:6), but we can thank God that Jesus is our advocate (1 John 2:1-2).**

friday • Zechariah 4:1-14

DIGGING DEEPER • In today's passage, Zechariah has a vision about the rebuilding of the temple. Joshua and Zerubbabel (the spiritual and civil rulers) are the two olive trees of that day that God would use to rebuild the temple. In verse 7 God promises to remove the obstacles that stand in their way. It would not be by human might or human power, but by God's Spirit, that the temple would be rebuilt. The oil represents the power of the Holy Spirit that would be poured out on them to accomplish God's work. Even though this temple was smaller than the original, the people were told it was not to be despised (v. 10). After all, the eyes of the Lord would see everything there and throughout the whole earth.

What work has the Lord given you to do? Remember: your abilities are all meaningless if you are not trusting God. Write out verse 6 and keep it with you.

saturday • Zechariah 5:1-11

DIGGING DEEPER • What comes to your mind when you hear the word *money*? Do you want more of it? Or do you fear it? The Israelites that were in Babylonian captivity began to love money and riches more than God. Zechariah has two visions in this passage. The first vision, in verses 1-4 gives us a picture of the holiness of God and His hatred for sin. Verses 5-11 talk of the evil that Satan wants to preserve on the earth. The woman in the basket is a picture of sin. The women with wings are returning her to Babylon. This vision is of the millennium, when sin will finally be wiped out from the earth, just as the people will be (v. 4) who harbor evil in their hearts.

We belong to Christ and sin has no power over us. Yet, every day we get to choose: Are we are going to live for God or for ourselves? It's your choice.

We have an exciting week of Bible study before us as we see the unfolding of God's plan for the Jewish people, Jerusalem, and the rest of the world. Watch and see this week how our faithful God has woven together the past, the present, and the future to fulfill His ultimate plan!

Week 36

prayer focus for this week

the Question the Answer

What is the writer saying?

How Can I apply this to my life?

sunday • Zechariah 6:1-8

Q

A

DIGGING DEEPER • Does discussion about the end times scare you? Maybe you find it just plain confusing? This vision is the eighth and final vision of Zechariah and is of the Kidron Valley: the place of final judgment on earth. The mountains are the Mount of Olives and Mount Zion. Zechariah sees four horse-drawn chariots. These four horses and chariots follow the pattern of the four horsemen of the Apocalypse found in Revelation 6. The "red" horse is representative of bloodshed; the "white" horse, victory; the "black" horse is famine and disease; and the "dappled" horse symbolizes death. These horses go out and bring judgment to the whole earth.

Those of us who know the Lord will be with Him during these final days of judgment on the earth. Are you ready to meet the Lord should you die today?

monday • Zechariah 6:9-15

DIGGING DEEPER • The next individual to wear the crown of David will be Jesus Christ when He establishes His kingdom here on earth during His millennial reign. In these verses Joshua represents Jesus, our Great High Priest. This ceremony was symbolic in order to show that the Messiah would be both a Priest and King. This whole passage prophetically shows how Christ will one day be crowned King of kings and Lord of lords. Jesus is our great High Priest, and He is sitting at the right hand of God, waiting for the time when He will return to establish His Kingdom here on earth.
Hebrews has a great deal to say about Jesus as High Priest. Take a look at Hebrews 7:27-28. Jesus has done what no other High Priest could: He paid the debt for all our sins!

tuesday • Zechariah 7:1-14

DIGGING DEEPER • Do you often find yourself just *going through the motions* in your walk with God? Today we read the first of four messages that Zechariah receives from the Lord. These are messages of warning against ritualistic, ceremonial, and heartless worship. While the Jewish people were in captivity, they had established some days of fasting in order to remember the days of national calamity. Now that they were no longer in captivity, they ask the priests if it is right to continue this ritual. The Scriptures do not tell us what the priests said, but we do read that God Himself wants to go beyond the issue of fasting and weighs their motives. God's concern was not whether they fasted or not, but why they fasted.
How is your time of worship? Is your spiritual life based on ritual or a heartfelt relationship with Him?

wednesday • Zechariah 8:1-13

DIGGING DEEPER • Do you ever think about God's ultimate plan? Despite violence and conflict in the world today, God has a plan for Israel and the rest of the world… and you! This chapter focuses on the great days the Lord has planned in Israel's future. It looks forward to a restored Jerusalem during the Millennium. Verse 8 refers to the day when the nation of Israel will turn back to the Lord and recognize Him as their Messiah. During this time, the Jewish people will return from the east and west (everywhere) to reside in Jerusalem. Verse 12 speaks of a future time when God will pour out blessings on Israel. **Do you feel like you've messed up God's plan for your life? It's not too late! God has a plan for you. Take some time today to confess your sin and get your heart right with God (1 John 1:9), and let Him take control!**

thursday • Zechariah 8:14-23

DIGGING DEEPER • Do you always tell the truth, or are you only honest when it is convenient? Half-truths are still lies. The Lord wants us to be truthful all the time! In verse 15, we see that God is going to show mercy to Israel. One day, the blessings of God will flow in Jerusalem and His judgment will cease. When the Bible speaks of fasting, it means to go without food for a period of time. The Jewish people had four fasts that were all in remembrance of the calamities that had come upon Jerusalem. Verses 16-17 are instructions for how God's people should live: in truth! We see in verses 18-19 that God will turn their fasting into feasting. **Have you moved from the fasting stage (repentance) to the feasting stage (joy) in your Christian life? When was the last time you rejoiced because of your salvation? Ask the Lord to restore to you the *joy of His salvation*.**

friday · Zechariah 9:1-9

DIGGING DEEPER · God cares about His people. He has and will continue to punish those who are enemies of Israel. The first eight verses here talk of judgment on Gentile nations. These verses were fulfilled by Alexander the Great. It was thought that the city of Tyre was indestructible. But, this city was conquered by Alexander the Great in 333 B.C. when he scraped the island city of Tyre flat, killing 2000 and enslaving 30,000 (v. 3-4). In verse 6, the Lord says He will "cut off the pride of the Philistines." They never became a nation again! All of these prophecies were fulfilled. Verse 9 tells of Christ's triumphant entry into Jerusalem on Palm Sunday. **In a world that doesn't believe in absolute truth and is swayed by new philosophies or ideas, we have a solid and firm foundation in Jesus Christ. God's Word is true and unchanging. His Word is living and powerful.**

saturday · Zechariah 9:10-17

DIGGING DEEPER · Are you ever shocked or scared by the events going on in the world around you? Nothing is a surprise to God. He not only knows what is going on in this world, but He is in control of it. In verse 10, the Lord says that the chariot, horses, and battle bow shall be cut off. There will be no need for Jerusalem to have these offensive weapons because Jesus has come to bring peace to the earth. In verse11, God is speaking to the suffering remnant that remains in Israel, referencing the Davidic and Abrahamic Covenants. God will restore prosperity to His people. The only deliverance for all mankind is through the shed blood of Christ. **There will be no peace on earth until Jesus returns and establishes it. Take some time today to pray for those in the middle of conflicts around the world and for the continued spread of the Gospel.**

How can an Old Testament prophetic book be beneficial to your life today? You'd be surprised! Fasten your seat belt as we move all the way through the 1000-year millennial reign of Christ. You will be amazed as you read this inspired Scripture written nearly 500 years before Christ's birth.

Week 37

prayer focus for this week

the Question
the Answer

What is the writer saying?

How can I apply this to my life?

sunday • Zechariah 10:1-12

Q

A

DIGGING DEEPER • Do you have things or people in your life that are more important to you than your relationship with God? An idol is anything that takes the place of God in your life. Idolatry was a problem in Israel, and verse 2 talks about the deceit of idolatry. "Oppressor" in verse 4 is better translated "ruler"; therefore, four beautiful pictures of Christ are seen in this verse: Christ the Cornerstone, Christ the Nail (see Isaiah 22:23-25), Christ our Battle Bow, and Christ the Ruler. The last seven verses here tell of how Christ will strengthen Israel and restore the nation. In verse 8, we see that He will call the Jews back home. **Today's events in the Middle East point to fulfillment of Bible prophecy. Christ could return today! Are you living as though you expect Him at any moment?**

monday • Zechariah 11:1-11

Q

A

DIGGING DEEPER • Have you ever been punished because of your disobedience? This is the case for Israel. The first six verses of this chapter tell of the terrible judgment that Israel will face for their rejection of their Messiah. This prophecy was fulfilled when the Romans attacked and destroyed Israel in 70 A.D. The three shepherds of verse 8 most likely refer to leaders of Zechariah's day whose spiritual corruption led to the extreme wickedness during the time of Christ. The breaking of the staff in verse 10 signifies that God is removing His favor from the nation of Israel because of their rejection of Him. Look closely... this was the breaking of a *conditional covenant* with Israel, not an unconditional one. The Lord's promise of protection for them was dependent upon their obedience to Him. **Take time to read about and meditate on the Shepherd who leads and restores you through all the trials of life (Psalm 23).**

tuesday • Zechariah 11:12-17

Q

A

DIGGING DEEPER • In these verses, Zechariah is acting out, not only a story, but a prophecy! It is likely that Zechariah was parading around in shepherd's garb acting out the story of the betrayal of Jesus. It is possible that someone threw 30 pieces of silver at him. This small amount of money signified what Israel felt Jesus was worth. Take another look at verse 12. Does it sound familiar? It was fulfilled when Judas betrayed Jesus for thirty pieces of silver, the price of a slave. After presenting The Good Shepherd, Zechariah presents the evil, or false shepherd: the Antichrist. The Jewish people are still scattered throughout the world today. But one day, God will restore the nation. **Is your walk with God genuine or just an imitation? Judas appeared to follow the Lord, but betrayed Him. Are you serious about God or only content in Him when it's convenient?**

wednesday • Zechariah 12:1-14

Q
A

DIGGING DEEPER · Have you ever hardened your heart against God? Did you know He was calling you to do something and you ignored Him? The "cup of trembling" in verse 2 means the Lord will pour out His wrath through Israel on the nations that rise against her. The Day of the Lord includes the Great Tribulation Period and the Millennial Kingdom. The remainder of this chapter tells of the future siege on Jerusalem. God will defend and protect the nation and destroy those who harm Israel. In verse 12 the people mourn for they understand that they have rejected their Savior and pierced Him. During this time, there will be a great outpouring of the Spirit in Jerusalem and great repentance and revival will come. **Have you experienced the forgiveness of your sins available through Christ's blood shed for you at the cross? Take time today to thank Jesus for paying the ultimate price for you.**

thursday • Zechariah 13:1-9

Q
A

DIGGING DEEPER · Take a good look at your hands. Now think of Jesus' hands and the nails that pierced through them. It was for you. If you have placed your trust in Him, He has forgiven you! The fountain of verse 1 represents forgiveness through Jesus' death and resurrection. Israel will be forgiven at the Second Coming of Christ, when the nation finally acknowledges Jesus as its Messiah. A fountain of cleansing will open up (John 19:32-37). Christ's sacrificial death on the cross will become real to those in Jerusalem who believe. Israel will ask Christ: "What are these wounds in thine hands?" (v. 6). The Jews will finally realize that Christ died for their sins. **In the end times, Israel will finally accept Jesus as their Savior. He is a merciful, loving, and gracious God. Not only has He saved you from your sins, but God takes care of you every day. Thank Him for it!**

friday • Zechariah 14:1-11

DIGGING DEEPER • Have you had a hard time understanding why God allows things to happen in your life? Life is not always easy, but God is always in control. It is now the end of the Tribulation and all the armies of the world are gathering against Jerusalem. In verse 3, we see what was already foretold in Zechariah 12:8-9: The Lord will crush the armies that harm Jerusalem. When Jesus returns He will literally stand on the Mount of Olives (v. 4). A great earthquake will split the Mount of Olives in two—right down the middle, forming a great, 40 mile plain with the temple exalted in the middle. A new river will run from Jerusalem to the Mediterranean Sea and the Dead Sea. Jesus Christ will reign over the whole earth and there will be no more destruction as people dwell safely in Jerusalem. **Christ is the central theme of history. One day every knee will bow. Why not worship Him now?**

saturday • Zechariah 14:12-21

DIGGING DEEPER • As we come to the end of this book, we see that the Lord will ultimately bring spiritual and physical deliverance to Israel. In the first several verses we see the plagues that come upon the enemies of God. All the spoils from victory will be left for Israel. Verse 16 speaks of the salvation of not only a remnant of Israel, but a remnant of each of the Gentile nations, as well. The nations will worship the Lord and keep the annual Feast of Tabernacles during the Millennium. We see in the last two verses that everything will be dedicated for the service of God. Everything will be "Holiness unto the Lord." Holiness will be the way of life here on earth. What a wonderful thing! **Are you willing to give whatever the Lord asks of you in order to use it for His service? What are you holding back from Him? Whatever it is, surrender it to God today.**

Do you really think God is big enough to handle all your problems? It might be easy for you to answer "yes" when everything is going fine. But how about when things aren't going so well? This week we'll discover that God is big enough for all our needs and far superior to anyone else, including angels.

Week 38

prayer focus for this week

the Question
the Answer

What is the writer saying?

How Can I apply this to my life?

sunday • Hebrews 1:1-7

Q
A

DIGGING DEEPER • Do you remember when you were a little kid and you brought something really cool to show your friends at school? You felt like the most popular kid in school until somebody else came in with something better. The writer of Hebrews is sharing a similar scenario. They had the prophets' teachings revealing how God wanted them to live, but the writer shows how Jesus is so much better than the prophets. Jesus is superior simply because He is the Creator of all things, and He now sits with authority above all that He has created.

How is Jesus described as being much superior to prophets and angels? Describe Jesus in a comparative way to great leaders, to politicians. List ways He is better.

monday • Hebrews 1:8-14

DIGGING DEEPER • Three are better than one! The Trinity is one of the most misunderstood doctrines in Scripture. When it comes to creation, the Father is represented by the architect; He planned it all. The Son executed the plans of the Father, as the contractor of the building. The Holy Spirit is represented by the various artisans who actually put the building together. When it comes to our salvation, the Father planned it in eternity past, the Son executed it at Calvary, and the Holy Spirit brought it to you at your conversion. God is so much superior to any of the other gods this original audience had encountered as well as any that we may come across today. **What other gods do people worship instead of the one true God? How do we put other things above God crowding Him out of our lives today?**

tuesday • Hebrews 2:1-9

DIGGING DEEPER • Have your parents ever explained something to you in agonizing detail? Maybe they wanted you to make sure you kept the stairway clear so your baby brother wouldn't trip and fall. However, you were too busy doing your own thing. Instead of listening, you ignored their instructions. In comes your brother at full speed, right into whatever it was you left on the stairs. He trips on it and gets hurt. It is at that time your parents remind you of the power of the spoken word. It is the same in this passage. The author is reminding us to pay attention to our salvation so we won't drift away from it and fail to grow. **Make a checklist of three things you should do daily to help you grow spiritually. Are reading the Bible and praying part of that list? How does God remind you of your forgetfulness to read His Word?**

wednesday • Hebrews 2:10-18

DIGGING DEEPER • You have probably known someone in school who was – well, a little bit different. Many times, there is someone who feels sorry for that person, talks to him, and does things with him. That someone goes out of his way just to make sure the "different" person doesn't feel left out or alone. He leaves the security of his own friends to make sure that everyone has a friend. Isn't that the way with Jesus? He's the Someone who left the treasures of Heaven to come down to earth just so we could have a relationship with Him. We are just like that poor kid in school. Sin separated us from God, but Jesus reached out to us when we were most pitiful.
How does God meet our needs? To whom is Jesus leading you to reach out?

thursday • Hebrews 3:1-6

DIGGING DEEPER • We have all been around people who seem to do no wrong. They always get the teacher's praise, the awards, and are the pride of their parents. Everything they touch seems to turn to gold. Doing right always has its rewards. God also blessed Moses for his obedience. Yet, even Moses needed to have faith in God. The author of Hebrews wants us to understand how ridiculous it is to compare ourselves with other people. The only One we should compare ourselves to is Jesus. Once we realize how far short we fall when compared to Him, we will be less likely to compare ourselves to others.
What are the characteristics that you admire most about your role models? What are some of the characteristics that you most admire about Jesus?

friday • Hebrews 3:7-13

DIGGING DEEPER • "Clean your room!" Perhaps you have heard that command hundreds of times. You have probably thought to yourself, "That just doesn't seem to make much sense. It will only get dirty again." What if we thought that about our walk with the Lord? This passage reminds us of the unfaithful Israelites who hardened their hearts toward the Lord. God blessed them by delivering them from the Egyptians, but they missed the blessings of the Promised Land!

Have you ever disobeyed your parents, thinking that you had gotten away with it, only to find out that in disobeying you missed out on something they were going to do for you? Is there anything hidden in your heart that is keeping you from a closer relationship with the Lord?

saturday • Hebrews 3:14-19

DIGGING DEEPER • Nathan raced for his birthday presents as soon as he walked in the door. Starting with the biggest ones, he tore through them at a frantic pace. Then he found the card that his grandparents gave him. He didn't even bother to open that. Later on the phone with Grandma, she asked if he liked his card, and he responded with a forced, "Oh, yeah." To which she replied that he should spend the $100 she placed in his card wisely! WOW, he had totally missed it! The stubborn Israelites were just like this selfish child on his birthday. God desires to give us so much more than we settle for. In our impatience, we take what we can get as long as we can have it *now*.

Name one thing that you just had to have right away. Name one thing for which you had to save money. Which did you appreciate more?

Have you ever needed encouragement to start talking to your friends about Jesus? The verses this week are just what you have been waiting for! We do not have all the time in the world to tell our friends about Christ. We should tell them now, before it is too late.

Week 39

prayer focus for this week

the Question
the Answer

What is the writer saying?

How Can I apply this to my life?

sunday • Hebrews 4:1-11

Q

A

DIGGING DEEPER • What happened to the fire we had when we were first saved? It seems to fade as we live our life of faith. Many times, we begin to try to live without God. God has more for us as we learn to depend on Him everyday. He promises that we will have rest for our souls if we trust in Him completely. This is where the Israelites failed. They quickly forgot the miracles God performed for them as He delivered them from bondage in Egypt. As a result, God led them into the wilderness. There would be many hard lessons to learn because of their disobedience. It would have been much easier if they would have only obeyed.

Why is it hard to depend on God's answer when you are experiencing trouble? Think of three ways that God has granted you rest by trusting in Him alone.

monday • Hebrews 4:12-16

DIGGING DEEPER • Do you ever feel like no one truly understands what you are going through? You may talk to your friends or even your parents, but you can tell by looking in their eyes that they just don't get it. Sure, they listen intently, but they don't understand. You really do have Someone who understands. Talk with Jesus in prayer. He understands exactly what you are going through. When He walked the earth, He faced the same struggles you are facing and successfully overcame them. He promises to give you help in time of trouble and whenever you have a need. He can be fully trusted. **Think of something that is troubling you right now… something that you can't talk about to anyone. Talk to Jesus about it. Search the Scriptures and write down three things that Jesus struggled with but overcame.**

tuesday • Hebrews 5:1-8

DIGGING DEEPER • "You just don't know how good you have it." Have you ever heard that expression before? Sure, only about every time your parents have asked you to do something and you have responded to them with less enthusiasm than they expected. Seriously, we do have it pretty good when we compare ourselves to the people in the Old Testament. They had to rely on the priests to offer sacrifices for them. We can actually talk directly to God. Jesus was the perfect sacrifice, one that doesn't need to be repeated. Once we accept His sacrifice, we are made completely clean and can speak directly to God. **Do you appreciate the privilege of speaking directly to God? Why not do it right now and thank Him for it!**

wednesday • Hebrews 5:9-14

DIGGING DEEPER • They say that you can't judge a book by its cover. The same can be said of those who claim to be Christians. We can accept Christ as our Savior, go to church, have our quiet time, and say our prayers. But is our salvation affecting our lives? If we have truly accepted Christ as our Savior, there should be a dramatic change in our lives. Things should be different. With the Holy Spirit within us, as we study the Word of God, we should understand more of what He wants us to do. It will also reveal things that He does not want us to do. The problem may be resistance to the work of the Word rather than lack of the Word. We aren't going to be perfect once we accept Jesus, but we should at least desire to be.
In what areas do you have a negative attitude? Is God truly in control of your life? He can do an excellent job with our attitude if we give it to Him.

thursday • Hebrews 6:1-8

DIGGING DEEPER • "Grow up!" Not exactly words you enjoy hearing. God encourages us to press on to maturity in our walk with Him. He doesn't expect us to lie around and soak up the blessings of salvation and not grow in our relationship with Him. Once we are saved, He expects us to grow. We should be like a tomato plant firmly rooted in good, fertilized, well-watered soil. We have no choice but to grow! If we fail to grow, God will cast us away like weeds in a summer garden. The more we resist God's voice in our lives, the less He will be able to use us. Our purpose is to come humbly before God with all that we have and allow Him to use us for His purpose.
What are your spiritual gifts? How can you use them to honor the Lord?

friday • Hebrews 6:9-15

DIGGING DEEPER • Why do we fidget so much when we have to stand and wait in a long line? Why is it a struggle to wait until Friday to get our allowance? It is lack of patience. We've heard it a million times, "Be patient," or "Good things come to those who wait." Have you ever thought that patience is a sign of maturity—physically and spiritually? Think about a hungry little baby. He doesn't know how to wait. He wants his food immediately. We're not babies; we shouldn't be impatient with God. Our walk with Him should continue to grow and mature, and there will be times when we just have to patiently wait.
The next time you have to wait in a check-out line, go to the longest one on purpose. Why do you think patience is so important to God?

saturday • Hebrews 6:16-20

DIGGING DEEPER • *Hope* may unofficially hold second place only to *love* as being the most overused word in the English language. We *hope* it won't rain during the game. We *hope* that we get an "A" on our school project. With such a watered-down sense of hope, it is hard to see exactly what the writer of Hebrews is trying to share with us. In our everyday conversations, we hope for what we do not have. However, as Scripture explains to us here, if we place our hope in the living Christ, we have a living hope. Our hope is in the here and now. We possess what we are hoping in; that is, we have a relationship with Jesus.
How is your hope in Jesus different than any other hope that you have? What do you think of when you think of hope?

Have you ever believed that the Old Testament was a waste of time to read or study? Hopefully this week's study of Scripture will change your mind. We are going to dig into some passages that show the importance of the Old Testament for us today.

Week 40

prayer focus for this week

the Question
the Answer

What is the writer saying?

How Can I apply this to my life?

sunday • Hebrews 7:1-10

Q

A

DIGGING DEEPER · Do you find contentment in having things around to enjoy? Do you enjoy giving your things away? You're probably thinking, "What planet did you come from? Why would giving things away be enjoyable?" In these verses, we read about Abraham offering the Lord's servant a tithe. This offering helped the Lord's servant continue doing the Lord's work. God enjoys giving us things. One thing we need to remember is not to be selfish with the things He provides. It isn't a sin to have things, but God desires that we share them. We should be open-handed with our possessions – excited to share them with others. We should never be reluctant givers, but give with a glad heart (2 Corinthians 9:7). **Name three things that you own that you feel you could never give up? Ask yourself why you couldn't. Are you putting too much importance on them?**

monday • Hebrews 7:11-17

DIGGING DEEPER · Have you ever thought of Jesus as a High Priest? What do you picture in your mind when you think of a High Priest? Maybe you think of the priests who were listening to the trumped up charges brought against our Lord before His crucifixion. Is this who the passage is referring to? No. The Old Testament law with its sacrificial system and priesthood could not save people. It could only give them a sense of how far they were from obeying it. A new system was necessary. Enter Jesus, our Great High Priest!

Offer praise to the Lord, our High Priest, who has offered before the Father all that is necessary for us to have a relationship with Him. Can you think of anyone to introduce Him to today?

tuesday • Hebrews 7:18-22

DIGGING DEEPER · "Nothing in life is guaranteed, except taxes and death," so the saying goes. When we live in the truth of Jesus' perfect sacrifice, we can be assured that we will inherit eternal life. Heaven is sure for us because Jesus' death and resurrection secured what God required for salvation. Being born sinners, we have nothing to offer a perfect, holy God that would allow Him to blot out our sins and transgressions. He paid it all! Think about that as you serve Him. Do not serve Him because of what you hope He will do for you, but because of what He has done for you. It's not about us; it's all about God. With God, it is definitely Who you know!

Name three things that are impossible for you to do alone, but with God's help you can do them.

wednesday • Hebrews 7:23-28

DIGGING DEEPER • Jesus, as High Priest, is altogether superior to the priests of the Old Testament. In fact, the Old Testament priests could only serve for a limited amount of time due to the nagging inconvenience of death. Not so with Jesus! He lives forever to intercede, or go to the Father on our behalf. Even when we do not know what to pray for or how to pray for a particular need, Jesus stands next to the Father sharing our needs with Him (Hebrews 7:25). He has no motive except our ultimate good. What an awesome God we serve!

What makes Jesus' sacrifice better than those of the Old Testament? Why did the Old Testament priests continue to offer sacrifices over and over?

thursday • Hebrews 8:1-6

DIGGING DEEPER • Have you ever read through some parts of the Old Testament and wondered what the point is in reading that stuff? Some of the Old Testament seems unfamiliar when it talks about animal sacrifices, sprinkling blood on door frames, and waving grain in the air! These were all symbolic of what Christ would do for us as our great High Priest. Once you understand the sacrifice that Jesus made for us, you can better appreciate all the details of the sacrifices explained in the Old Testament. This is just one more reason we should stop what we are doing in our busy day and thank God for what He has given to us so freely.

Name three duties of a High Priest. How are the promises offered by Jesus better than the ones offered in the Old Testament?

friday • Hebrews 8:7-13

DIGGING DEEPER • Have you ever watched TV commercials that introduce a "new and improved" product? What are they trying to say? Was the old version worthless? No. They make these new claims so as to encourage us to purchase their *new* product. As we read these verses in Hebrews, it would appear that the writer is telling us that God is doing something similar with the New Covenant. But that isn't what He is saying at all. The author of Hebrews wants to show us that, in the Old Testament, the Law shows us how far off track we are. The New Testament gives us hope by giving us a new heart. God gave us the very thing we needed in order to gain His favor – His Son.

What is a covenant? How have you benefited from the New Covenant made by Jesus dying on the cross?

saturday • Hebrews 9:1-10

DIGGING DEEPER • Have you ever gone to an amusement park with a friend? Perhaps you wanted to go on a ride together, but you were too short. No matter how you stretched your neck, you still were not tall enough. This scenario is similar to how it used to be in Old Testament times. God did not allow just anyone to come into the Temple and enter into His presence. The priest was only permitted to go in once a year. But now, all of that has changed. Jesus made all the difference. Now we can all enter into the Lord's presence through the finished work of Christ, and we can do it anytime we want!

Take time now to thank the Lord for letting you come to Him with every need that you have. What need is burdening your heart today? Share it with Him.

Have you ever read portions of the Old Testament and thought to yourself, "What is up with all of the animal sacrifices?" Hopefully, as we undertake our studies this week, that question will be answered. As you carefully read these verses, be attentive for words like sacrifice, cleansed, and forgiveness.

Week 41

prayer focus for this week

the Question
the Answer

What is the writer saying?

How Can I apply this to my life?

sunday · Hebrews 9:11-15

Q

A

DIGGING DEEPER · Completely. Totally. Once-for-all. These are words that describe what Christ's sacrifice did for us when it comes to payment for our sin. The blood of imperfect animal sacrifices had to be offered by imperfect priests daily in order to atone for man's sins. Jesus, the perfect High Priest, was the spotless sacrifice making it unnecessary for man to offer anything else. Our debt for all the sins we have committed in the past, present, and even in the future, has been paid in full by the sacrifice of Jesus' death and resurrection.

Why did Jesus only have to offer Himself once as a sacrifice while the Old Testament priest had to offer sacrifices more often? Can you think of a friend that needs to hear of this Good News?

monday • Hebrews 9:16-22

DIGGING DEEPER · "If you get straight A's on your report card, you can choose any place you would like to go on your birthday," your dad says. Wow! Wouldn't that be exciting! But, your excitement soon fades as you remember chemistry, physics, and history. As the year wears on, your grades are like a submarine; they drop below "C" level. You begin to get discouraged. What if someone offered to take your place and that someone could get A's in your classes? That's what Jesus did for us, not in chemistry, physics, or history, but in real life. God demands perfection. We could never measure up. Jesus could and did! He became our substitute and because of His shed blood, we can find forgiveness in Him. We win!

The New Covenant (Testament) was sealed by Christ's blood. What does that mean to you if you've trusted Him as your Savior?

tuesday • Hebrews 9:23-28

DIGGING DEEPER · Do you realize that when you placed your faith in Christ, He delivered you from the penalty of sin (past), the power of sin (present), and that one day in the future He will even deliver you from the very presence of sin? Why is that? Because once we have placed our faith in Jesus, God looks at us through Jesus' blood and sees us as blameless. Isn't that an awesome thought? You have been identified as a child of God. What a wonderful privilege! We can benefit from uninterrupted fellowship with God because of Jesus' death. The same way that Jesus talks to God, so can we!

Christ kept our appointment with death for us and there is no more condemnation. Do you look forward to your daily appointment with Him in your quiet time for a time of communion?

wednesday • Hebrews 10:1-10

Q
A

DIGGING DEEPER • Why all the sacrifices? In our passage today we see why those details were recorded for us. In Hebrews, the author shows us how Jesus was a perfect sacrifice and substitute. He only had to die once for all our sins since He had no sin of His own. He was sinless. The Old Testament priests had to continually offer sacrifices because they were just as sinful as the people. All we need to do is trust in Jesus as our Savior and accept His gift of eternal life. God then accepts us into His family.
Have you made that decision yet to trust Him as your Savior? If you are saved, list a couple of ways you can show your love for the Lord or others.

thursday • Hebrews 10:11-18

Q
A

DIGGING DEEPER • Have you ever had the pleasure of eating rotten meat? Mmmm! Let's add a whole bunch of salt, pepper, onions, garlic, and oregano. Would that take care of it? Yuk! Of course not! All of those extra ingredients would merely cover up the rotten meat. It wouldn't make it fresh again. It's kind of what our passage is saying here today. The Old Testament sacrifices never actually took away anyone's sins. That's why they had to be offered over and over again. There wasn't even a place for the High Priest to sit down because his work was never done. But Jesus' sacrifice of Himself was sufficient and only had to be offered once. Now He is seated at the right hand of God and intercedes for us!
Since our sins and iniquities will be remembered no more, why not offer a prayer of thanksgiving? Pray for someone that needs the Lord.

friday • Hebrews 10:19-25

DIGGING DEEPER • Honestly, there may be many times when you question the importance of going to church every week. I mean, after all, isn't it enough that you are saved, read your Bible, and pray everyday? Verse 25 of our Scripture reading for the day seems to answer our question. The Lord desires us to accept Him as our Savior, but He also wants us to spread the Good News. He knows our hearts. By coming together each week we can encourage one another, pray for one another, grow together, and join other believers in witnessing, praising, and worshipping Him.

How important is regular church attendance to you? What other benefits can you gain from going to church regularly?

saturday • Hebrews 10:26-31

DIGGING DEEPER • Appreciation. Respect. Thankfulness. These three words should come quickly to mind when someone does something for you that you did not earn or deserve. We should be especially mindful of all the Lord has done for us. Just imagine what it would be like without God's blessings on our lives. We must continue to not take God for granted and remember to give Him thanks for all He continues to do for us. If not, God will gradually remove His blessings to help us remember. If that doesn't work, He will eventually judge us for our ingratitude and thoughtlessness.

List three things that God has accomplished in your life recently. List three ways you have shown your appreciation to the Lord lately.

Where does your hope lie? What is faith? In whom do you have faith? Faith in Jesus as your personal Lord and Savior is just the beginning of your journey in His family. God desires that we also use that faith in our daily walk with Him. This week we will learn how to trust in Him, realizing He knows what's best for us.

prayer focus for this week

the Question
the Answer

What is the writer saying?

How Can I apply this to my life?

sunday · Hebrews 10:32-39

Q
A

DIGGING DEEPER · Do bad things ever happen to good people? What about to Christians? Of course they do. Since we know that God knows all things and that nothing happens without His permission, why does God allow bad things to happen? This passage helps us partially understand God's reasoning. When we endure hardships by trusting God and obeying His will for our lives, we will receive what God has promised. This is far better than giving up and trying to do things our own way. The Bible is full of examples of people who tried to do things their own way only to regret the outcome. As the songwriter says, it's best when we "trust and obey."

Can you think of an instance when you trusted God through a bad time? Can you think of someone who is going through a difficult time? Perhaps God wants you to share with someone how He has been faithful in your life.

monday • Hebrews 11:1-6

DIGGING DEEPER · What is faith? We tend to throw that word around a lot. But, do we truly know or understand what it means to have faith in Jesus? Faith is simply knowing or understanding something to be true. We have faith in Jesus, not just because of the miracles He performed, but because those deeds help us see that all He has said and done is true. If we really want to experience God's blessing, we must place our faith and trust in Him both for our daily walk and when it comes to our future. After all, He's the One who knows the future and He is our trustworthy Guide.
What can you do that will become a walk of faith? List two things you will trust God for this week.

tuesday • Hebrews 11:7-12

DIGGING DEEPER · Abel revealed his faith by his *worship*, Enoch showed his faith by his *walk*, and Noah demonstrated it through his *work*. Each was different but they all demonstrated a right relationship with the Lord. It's always encouraging to hear of those who have gone before us through hardships, yet remained faithful to the Lord. One thing about our faith that should strengthen and comfort us is the fact that no matter what happens to us as believers, we will never suffer God's wrath. Since we have accepted Christ as our Savior, we are under the divine protection and shielding of the Lord. Now that's security!
Which of the three do you best identify with: *worship*, *walk*, or *work*? Would others agree with your assessment of yourself?

wednesday • Hebrews 11:13-19

DIGGING DEEPER • Is this as good as it gets? Thank the Lord, it is NOT! It is sad and depressing to see people put all their hope and dreams into efforts that won't last, or to see them invest in things with little or no eternal value. As believers, we must use our God-given faith to supernaturally "see" beyond this temporary home that we call earth and catch a glimpse of our eternal home in Heaven. It is there that we should place our hope. That is the sure foundation that can satisfy our deepest needs. If the Old Testament saints could exercise faith having so little of God's Word, how much more should we now that we have a complete Bible?
Where are you placing your hope and trust? If it is in the Lord, it's a safe investment and one that is certain to pay rich dividends.

thursday • Hebrews 11:20-29

DIGGING DEEPER • Another important characteristic of our new *eyes of faith* is that they help us see beyond life's difficulties and teach us to trust the Lord's strength in our time of need. There may be times when things don't seem to make sense or that fairness and justice are not prevailing, but these were never promised to us. Faith allows us to choose the difficult, yet right thing to do over the easy path. Although there may be many times we fail, God continues to be faithful and patient with us. Keep your *eyes of faith* fixed on Him and never turn to the left or right. We often needlessly suffer because we take our eyes off Him.
It's important to keep our *eyes of faith* focused on the Lord rather than on self or man. List two things that you have trusted the Lord for in the last two weeks.

friday • Hebrews 11:30-35

DIGGING DEEPER • One of the most awesome things about the Bible is that it includes stories of common people – people like you and me. It reveals not only their successes, but, more importantly, their failures. God didn't necessarily use gifted, talented, or successful people to carry out His eternal plans. He chose people whom others considered unworthy and useless to accomplish His life-changing plans and ministry. This further illustrates His complete control of all of life's circumstances. The events recorded here go far beyond mere human capabilities. Jesus said, ... *greater works than these shall he do* (John 14:12). We can expect some great things, but we must be willing to attempt great things! **How has God been able to use you lately? What were the results? What can you do to increase your effectiveness?**

saturday • Hebrews 11:36-40

DIGGING DEEPER • All those listed in this passage went through great suffering to share their faith in God with others. Faith is one of the most powerful testimonies we can share. Do you struggle to find just the right words to share when witnessing? Do you feel scared or inadequate? Is it hard to muster up the courage to begin a conversation about spiritual things? Our personal testimonies of faith are so important. Whether you realize it or not, we *preach* a sermon everyday. We may not be behind a pulpit in church, but our actions, attitudes, reactions, and words all reflect the faith, or lack of faith that is in our hearts. We are witnesses to a watching, critical, and unbelieving world. What do they see? **You are being watched. Pray for an opportunity to witness of your faith today and ask the Lord for strength to give others the Gospel message.**

What would Jesus do? I know we have all heard that expression a million times, but it seems so important in our walk with the Lord. If we really want a deep, thriving relationship with Jesus, that question needs to run constantly through our minds. As you read this week's passages, think on these words.

prayer focus for this week

the Question
the Answer

What is the writer saying?

How can I apply this to my life?

sunday • Hebrews 12:1-8

Q

A

DIGGING DEEPER • Hard times are so much easier to endure when we have genuine friends cheering us on and encouraging us. We are often unaware of the power of sin. How easy it is for us to become distracted and fall. The author of Hebrews relates our Christian walk to a race. To move swiftly and smoothly, a successful runner must remove all that may get in his way. So it is with our walk with Christ. In order to grow more like Christ, we must avoid anything that hinders us or slows us down. He wants us to grow and go!

List three things in your Christian life that slow down your growth process. Which one of these will you work on this week to help you grow and go faster?

monday • Hebrews 12:9-15

DIGGING DEEPER • Who enjoys discipline? If we were disciplined more often, would we be happier? If you enjoy discipline, you're strange! However, let's distinguish between punishment (punitive) and discipline (preventative). Punishment is correction (remedial, from which we get the word remedy) when we have done something wrong. Discipline is used in order to teach us the importance of choosing what is best rather than settling for something less. Let's listen with an open heart to God's instructions as He teaches us to be more like Him. While discipline may not be fun, it helps us grow and become more like Jesus.

What are some of the things that discipline teaches us? In what ways has God disciplined you? How has it changed the way you live your life?

tuesday • Hebrews 12:16-24

DIGGING DEEPER • We all make decisions everyday. Some of them are important; others are not so important. Some decisions are between what is right and what is wrong. Then we must make decisions between what is good and what is best. The earth, which God created, is good. However, God did not create it to be worshipped, only as a clear testimony to Him. It should lead us to worship the One who created it. It is the same way when you see a beautiful house. You can stand and gaze upon its beauty, but when you meet the one who designed it, he is the one who is worthy of the praise for its creation and splendor. When it comes to creation of life and its splendor, it would be God who is worthy of praise.

Are you guilty of worshiping what God has given rather than God Himself? Your choices are important. Choose wisely today!

wednesday • Hebrews 12:25-29

DIGGING DEEPER · Have you ever received a really cool gift that included a huge instruction manual? After opening the package, you were so excited about your nice gift that you just tossed the instructions aside believing you could figure out the assembly and usage of it all by yourself. Then five hours later, you are sitting with an object in front of you that in no way resembles the picture on the front of the package. God has also given us a detailed set of instructions when it comes to life—the Bible. How does your life compare as you read it? Does your life resemble the One within its pages, or a thing created without reference to the instructions?

How do you read the Bible, quickly or slowly? Be honest, do you even read it? How do you want God to listen to your deepest heartfelt prayers?

thursday • Hebrews 13:1-8

DIGGING DEEPER · Materialism is all around us. Everywhere we look, someone is promoting something we just cannot live without. What should our attitude be toward possessions? God knows what we need and wants us to be content with what we have (v. 5). Our world is preaching a very different message today. It tells us not to be content. It says we should look out for ourselves and do all we can to get to the top. No wonder the simple message of the Gospel proves to be a stumbling block to some. But, for those who believe, it's a saving message. Contentment comes in Who we have, not what we have.

Jesus can see all the things you buy with your money. Do you think He is pleased with your choices?

friday • Hebrews 13:9-14

DIGGING DEEPER • A key thought that runs through other books of the Bible is, *Do not be deceived by false teachings.* With so many who teach false doctrines, it is important that we learn *why* we believe *what* we believe. We must be able to answer the questions that may arise from those who do not understand why we believe in Jesus and not in another religion. As we develop a good grasp of God's Word and understand what it says, we will be better equipped to answer any questions they might have. It may also enable us to give an answer that will meet a need in their life.

What are some false teachings we hear today? How would you describe faith to an unbeliever? If someone asked you, could you give them a clear presentation of your personal testimony? How about the Gospel?

saturday • Hebrews 13:15-25

DIGGING DEEPER • Do we still need to offer sacrifices to God in order to receive His forgiveness and blessing? Not in the same way as those in Old Testament times. The temple priests offered animal sacrifices. But in our passage today, the author tells us that we should offer sacrifices of praise to the Lord. This is done from a heart overflowing with thankfulness to God for all He has done and continues to do for us. In our devotion time, it's part of the ACTS method of quiet time: Adoration, Confession, THANKGSIVING, and Supplication. Let's be thankful today.

Choose a Psalm and personalize it to offer a sacrifice of praise to the Lord. What *good* thing (v. 16) can you do today that will bring honor and glory to the Lord?

When you think of 1 Corinthians you probably think of the love chapter. However, 1 Corinthians 13 is just one part of a letter from Paul to a messed up church. The church in Corinth had many problems, and Paul's goal in this letter is to address as many of those problems as he possibly can.

Week 44

prayer focus for this week

the Question the Answer

What is the writer saying?

How Can I apply this to my life?

sunday • 1 Corinthians 1:1-9

Q

A

DIGGING DEEPER • Aren't you glad God is faithful? Even when we deliberately disobey Him, He doesn't give up on us. Even when we clearly rebel against Him, He doesn't abandon us. Even when we absolutely ignore His Word, He doesn't... you get the point. If not, the point is that even when we're at the point of giving up on God, forgetting our faith, or dropping out of church, God remains absolutely faithful to us. Paul said it well when he said: *God is faithful* (v. 9). Our God really is a faithful God and He absolutely deserves our faithfulness in return. So let's give thanks to our faithful God and live our lives to honor Him.

When was the last time you thanked God for His faithfulness? How faithful have you been lately?

monday • 1 Corinthians 1:10-17

DIGGIHG DEEPER · Have you ever been a part of a church where no one seemed to be able to get along? If so, you're not alone. There are thousands of churches all over the world putting up with divisive people and their divisive issues. It's not a new problem. The Christians in Corinth had their own share of *divisions* (v. 10) much like many churches do today. While Paul doesn't go into all the details, this church obviously had a lot of arguing and fighting going on. What the Corinthian Christians didn't realize, and what our churches today often fail to realize, is that God hates division in the church. On top of that, division brings shame to the name of Christ!
Are you someone who causes division or brings about unity?

tuesday • 1 Corinthians 1:18-31

DIGGIHG DEEPER · The Gospel seems so trivial, foolish, and unimportant to those outside the faith. They think it's foolish to believe that Jesus lived a sinless life, paid the penalty for our sins on a cross, and three days after dying, rose from the grave. However, to us who have experienced Christ's love and forgiveness personally, the Gospel is much more than some fanciful fairy tale. It is life and truth! It is far from unimportant. Just as Israel had miraculously been delivered, God also delivers us. His Word is the truth that has set us free spiritually (John 8:32). In fact, it is of utmost importance; so much so, that we cannot keep from sharing it with everyone we know because it is the best news ever!
What makes the Gospel or *Good News* so good?

wednesday • 1 Corinthians 2:1-8

DIGGING DEEPER • Wouldn't it be great to have God speak through you? Wouldn't it be great to be used in this way? Paul experienced it firsthand during his ministry to the people of Corinth. As he stopped in Corinth on one of his missionary trips, Paul says he didn't write a speech, design a talk, or prepare a sermon for this occasion. No, in fact, he says that God's Spirit gave him the exact words he needed to say and that he wasn't about to ruin that with his own words, thoughts, or ideas. Like Paul, it would be good for us to let God's Holy Spirit have His way with our lives and mouths in whatever situation we may find ourselves.

What do you think it would be like to have God speak through you? What do you think it would take for that to happen?

thursday • 1 Corinthians 2:9-16

DIGGING DEEPER • What does it mean to have the mind of Christ? It's obvious we have the mind of Christ if we're saved (v. 16), but what exactly is it? To have the mind of Christ means to think like He thought. When we have the mind of Christ, we'll begin to think about lost people the same way Jesus did. When we have the mind of Christ, we'll begin to think more about loving our parents, loving our friends, and even loving our enemies. When we have the mind of Christ, we'll speak the words of Christ, live the life of Christ, and share the love of Christ! In summary, to have the mind of Christ is to be like Christ in our character, words, and actions.

Do you have the mind of Christ? How would your life be different if you lived out having the mind of Christ?

friday • 1 Corinthians 3:1-8

DIGGING DEEPER · Taking care of a baby is hard work! It seems like you are constantly feeding him, soothing him during a crying episode, or worst of all, changing his dirty diaper. It's a lot of work, right? As a result, it can be potentially frustrating. Now, imagine an adult who acts like a baby. He needs to be fed every two hours, takes four naps a day, and won't be quiet unless you stick a pacifier in his mouth. Now that would be a problem, wouldn't it? More than that, it would be really weird! Nevertheless, this is what Paul sees in the church of Corinth—Christians who haven't grown up! Paul addresses these immature believers as babies who need to put their pacifiers down, take their bibs off, drop their bottles, and start growing up as Christians.
In what ways and areas do you need to grow up as a Christian?

saturday • 1 Corinthians 3:9-15

DIGGING DEEPER · What are you doing that will last forever? What building materials are you using in your life? Some use wood, hay, or stubble while others use gold, silver, and precious stones. Sometimes things like text messaging, trips to the mall, and telephone conversations take up a lot of our time, but what are we doing that really matters? One day we will stand before our great and holy God and He will do a rigorous and thorough inspection of our lives. Only what's done for His name's sake will ultimately last and matter. So, here's the important question again—what are you doing that really matters?
How much time do you spend on temporary things in an average day? What could you do today that would make a difference in eternity?

Sometimes it helps to have someone talk to you plainly about mistakes you've made or sins you've committed. Paul continues his letter by addressing specific sins that seem to trap the Corinthian Christians. Pay close attention as these sins are still prevalent in the church, if not in our own lives as well.

Week 45

prayer focus for this week

the Question
the Answer

What is the writer saying?

How Can I apply this to my life?

sunday • 1 Corinthians 3:16-23

Q

A

DIGGING DEEPER • God lives in you. We are His temple. How cool is that? Think about it for just a minute. The Holy Spirit Himself lives in you! When we fully let this truth sink into our lives, what kind of difference will it make? It will certainly affect the places we go and the people with whom we hang out. It will probably affect the relationship we have with our parents. It will most likely change how frequently we open God's Word and how much time we spend listening and talking to Him. The truth is, it should affect every aspect of our lives! God really does live in you and it might be helpful for you to just write down *God lives in me* on an index card and put it somewhere where you'll see it and be reminded of it often.
Can your friends and family tell that God lives in you?

monday • 1 Corinthians 4:1-13

Q

A

DIGGIHG DEEPER • Have you ever used the phrase: *God knows my heart?* We normally use this phrase when someone has accused us of wrongdoing or suggested that we've been deceitful in some area. We use the phrase defensively to let them know that whether they believe us or not, God knows the attitude behind everything we just said or did. While we may not realize it on a daily basis, God really does know our hearts. He knows our secret thoughts and sees our shameful behavior. We don't stand a chance of hiding from Him. One day, according to verse 5, He'll bring our deepest and darkest moments to light and expose us for what we really are. We would do well to remember that we are humble servants.
How's your heart? Are you ready to stand before God?

tuesday • 1 Corinthians 4:14-21

Q

A

DIGGIHG DEEPER • We appreciate truth tellers. We're thankful for the people in our lives who give it to us straight. While we may not always appreciate that rebuke or that correction when it happens, we always end up appreciating it later. Truth tellers are valuable and everybody needs at least one of them in his life. Paul was a truth teller and while he writes the Corinthians in love, there's plenty of power to his words. In fact, as this letter unfolds, Paul speaks as plainly as any writer of Scripture does, addressing such topics as immorality, lawsuits, and marriage. He doesn't back down as he confronts the Corinthian Christians directly concerning their sin, but instead he gives it to them straight.
Do you have any truth tellers in your life who will give it to you straight?

wednesday • 1 Corinthians 5:1-13

DIGGING DEEPER • Are you hanging around Christians who are regularly disobeying God? If so, get away from them as quickly as you can. You must avoid them at all costs! Now, we're not saying that you need to avoid non-Christians who don't know any better. How can we possibly reach the lost if we don't know anybody who is lost? To some extent, we must hang around people who don't know Christ. The problem comes when we associate with Christians who know better, but choose to rebel against God. Paul says that the Christians who live like the world are the ones we need to avoid. Their bad habits easily could rub off on us.
Who do you need to stay away from until he begins to follow Christ again as he should?

thursday • 1 Corinthians 6:1-11

DIGGING DEEPER • We need to be known as the kind of people who are *passed our past*. As Paul gives us a list of dangerous sins, he adds these words: *and such were some of you* (v. 11). The key word in that sentence is, obviously, *were*. It's not such *are* some of you, but such *were* some of you. So what made the difference? Well, we could use the doctrinal words, *justification* or *sanctification* to describe what took place in their lives. The bottom line is that Jesus made the difference! He still makes all the difference in the world today. He can take the worst situation imaginable in our lives today and one day say to us *such were some of you* about the great change He brought about in our lives.
How has God changed your life up to this point? How are you different?

friday • 1 Corinthians 6:12-20

DIGGING DEEPER • There are some verses in the Bible that just make us say, *Wow!* 1 Corinthians 6:19 is one of those verses. When we read that the Holy Spirit lives inside us it just blows our mind! Think about this for a minute. The very God who created the universe and everything in it also lives in you in the person of the Holy Spirit. It's certainly a little difficult to swallow, but we come to the conclusion that it's true. God lives in us. Because He does, we have a responsibility to live our lives as if He were with us at all times because, the fact of the matter is, He is! This means that the sinful, sexual desires of the flesh need to be taken seriously and need to be brought into subjection to God's will and not our own.
What difference does it make that God lives in you? What areas of your life do you need to surrender to Him?

saturday • 1 Corinthians 7:1-9

DIGGING DEEPER • Marriage is a good thing. Actually, it's more that—it's a *God* thing. God instituted marriage way back in the Garden of Eden. He even said, *It is not good that the man should be alone* (Gen. 2:18). Paul obviously agrees with God, and adds that if a man loves a woman, *it is better to marry than to burn* with passion for her (v. 9). Paul is directly confronting yet another problem in the church at Corinth, specifically, sexual immorality. Paul's solution was a simple one—get married and be committed to each other. This command is equally applicable today. The church needs husbands and wives who will take their marriages seriously and be committed to one another for life.
Why is it important to stay pure in your dating? Why does God have such strict guidelines when it comes to sexual purity?

When God speaks, we must listen. We must never get to the place where we ignore His promptings and quit reading His Word. God wants to speak to us just as He wanted to speak to the Corinthians, and we must be open to the same truths and principles that He revealed to them.

prayer focus for this week

the Question
the Answer

What is the writer saying?

How Can I apply this to my life?

sunday • 1 Corinthians 7:10-24

Q

A

DIGGING DEEPER • Marriage is for life! Divorce should not be in the Christian's vocabulary. Unfortunately, we live in a world where divorce is unbelievably rampant and even accepted as normal. Perhaps the saddest part is that the Christians in our churches seem to be just as prone to divorce as men and women outside the church. God made marriage for keeps, and to have couples divorcing over pets, chores, and finances is ridiculous. We must understand that marriage was designed to be *'til death do us part*. There are no *escape clauses* in marriage vows and they are made to God, not just to mortal man.

Why do you think God hates to see a divorce take place? Why is it so important to stay married?

monday • 1 Corinthians 7:25-40

DIGGING DEEPER · One advantage that a Christian has in remaining single for his whole life is that he can be *sold out* to God. He can serve and minister in ways that a married man would find impossible. Obviously, the single person's concern would not be for his spouse or his kids as in the case of a married man. Therefore, his focus as a single person could be on pleasing God and God alone. His life can be a life lived for the glory of God. Now, let me be perfectly clear, this doesn't make marriage a bad thing. It just means that being single doesn't have to be a bad thing, and in fact, has the potential to be an awesome thing. While you're still single, why not give God all aspects of your life? It will be an investment that pays rich dividends.
Have you ever considered being single as a possibility for your future? Are you willing to pray about that?

tuesday • 1 Corinthians 8:1-13

DIGGING DEEPER · Although we who are Christians have freedom and liberty in our lives, we must be very careful not to live in such a way as to cause a younger, newer Christian to turn back to his old habits and hang-ups. Even though we may engage in an activity with a clear conscience, and with no sin in our hearts, we could hurt a Christian who is new to the faith by our behavior. We must be careful to be above reproach in our daily lives. While we ourselves can walk in absolute liberty, we must continually be aware that others could be hurt by our actions and choices. What may be acceptable for you, might be a stumbling block to a new believer.
Are you willing to give up your freedom so as to not do something that might negatively affect another Christian?

wednesday • 1 Corinthians 9:1-10

DIGGING DEEPER · *Am I not free* (v. 1)? What a great question! Perhaps we should think about using this question periodically in our own lives. The next time someone says, *Why are you wearing sandals in December?* we can just reply, *Are we not free?* Of course, Paul wasn't talking about that kind of freedom necessarily, but he was saying that, even though he was an apostle and missionary with his share of responsibility, he was free in Christ like everyone else. He wasn't bound to some man-made set of rules. The same is true for us! We don't have to be enslaved by a bunch of rules that aren't for us. We're free—free to obey Christ.

What does it mean for a Christian to be free? Are you free? Are you willing to surrender your liberty in certain activities so fellow believers will not stumble?

thursday • 1 Corinthians 9:11-18

DIGGING DEEPER · Your pastor deserves a paycheck! The Apostle Paul spells it out very clearly that it's not wrong for a pastor, missionary, or evangelist to get paid for what they do to help the church. In fact, it's not only acceptable, it's strongly encouraged. Although Paul himself didn't accept any money for doing what he was doing as a missionary to Corinth, he says that it's more than appropriate to pay those who lead the church. While you may think your pastor doesn't do anything but sit around the church and study, nothing could be further from the truth. So again, pay your pastor, but more than that, love him, and pray for him.

Do you appreciate all that your pastor does? When was the last time you told him thanks, sent him a card of appreciation, or prayed for him?

friday • 1 Corinthians 9:19-27

DIGGING DEEPER • Are you willing to do whatever it takes to see the people in your life accept God's forgiveness and surrender their lives to Christ? Paul said that he was willing to do anything that didn't violate Scripture to reach someone with the Gospel. He said, *I am made all things to all men, that I might by all means save some* (v. 22). Paul reached people by meeting men and women right where they were. He didn't say, *My way or the highway* when it came to ministry. He adapted to his audience. We could learn a lot from his example as we strive to share Christ with those we know. It involves self-denial and self-control.
Are you willing to do whatever it takes to see people in your life accept God's forgiveness and surrender their lives to Christ?

saturday • 1 Corinthians 10:1-11

DIGGING DEEPER • No grumbling allowed! This announcement would be a good one for us to make from time to time in our churches on Sunday. For whatever reason, the church can become a place of grumbling and complaining. Now, grumbling is not a good thing. In fact, just say the word *grumble* aloud three or four times and you'll see that it even sounds bad. Among many other prohibitions Paul mentions as he writes to the Corinthian Christians, he makes sure to include, *No grumbling allowed*! The actual word Paul uses is *murmur* – a double groan of nonsense that means the same thing as grumbling or complaining. The bottom line is that murmuring, complaining, and grumbling have no place in the church or in your life!
Are you someone who complains a lot? What could you do instead?

Satan hates the church! He will use whatever he can to disrupt, divide, and destroy it. Therefore, the church must be awake and aware by not giving in to the various temptations that come to us as individuals, or the church as a whole.

Week 47

prayer focus for this week

the Question / the Answer

What is the writer saying?

How Can I apply this to my life?

sunday • 1 Corinthians 10:12-22

Q

A

DIGGING DEEPER • Temptation is tough! Some would be *tempted* to say that temptation is easy to ignore, but that's just not true. Some would be tempted to say that they've never been tempted, but that would be an outright lie. Temptation, when it happens (and it happens very often), is tough to deal with. For instance, we're often *tempted* to put down our pencil, write a note, or play a game, instead of doing our quiet time, because everything within us says we deserve a break today. However, we must not listen to temptation. As soothing as its voice is, in the end, it brings nothing but pain and misery. God has promised a way of escape with every temptation we face. Expect it ... and look for it!

How do you deal with temptation? Do you give in? Do you trust God to help you?

monday • 1 Corinthians 10:23-33

DIGGING DEEPER • 1 Corinthians 10:31 is often one of the first verses we are encouraged to memorize because it will help us establish priorities in our lives. *Whether therefore ye eat, or drink, or whatsoever ye do, do all to the glory of God.* What a great verse! Did you know that when you're eating, it's possible to eat for God's glory? And when you go fishing, it's possible for you to do it for God's glory. And when you're reading, playing an instrument, competing in sports, or going for a jog, you can do all of these activities for God's glory. We could go on, and on, and on, but you get the point. Whatever you do, be sure that you are doing it for God's glory—not your own or anyone else's.
What do you need to start doing for God's glory? Are there any gray areas that need to be turned over to Him?

tuesday • 1 Corinthians 11:1-10

DIGGING DEEPER • Look at me! This is Paul's advice to those who just aren't sure how to live the Christian life on their own. In continuing his instructions to the Corinthian church, Paul says, *Follow me, Watch me,* or *Imitate me.* That's what he means when he says, *Be ye followers of me, even as I also am of Christ* (v. 1). He says this, not because he thinks he's the best role model ever (although he is a great role model), but because he is following, watching, and imitating Christ. Following Christ carries over into married life as well. In all relationships in life there has to be some type of submission. God the Father and God the Son are equal in essence, yet the Father is the head over Christ (v. 3). This is a great illustration.
Who are the men and women of God you look up to? What have you learned from them about following Christ?

wednesday • 1 Corinthians 11:11-22

Q

A

DIGGING DEEPER • Why can't we all just get along? Have you ever been in church and asked yourself that question? Unity is a word that should describe the churches where we worship. However, disunity is often the word that most accurately describes many of our churches. Think about this for a minute. If we all love Jesus, and we all worship the one and only God, and if we desire to live by the Holy Spirit's power, what's the problem? The problem is that we often don't love Jesus enough. We get caught up with *issues* that take our attention off the Lord, and we don't depend on the Holy Spirit to guide us in the Christian life. So let's do something different for a change. Let's get along!

How can you contribute to a spirit of unity in your church?

thursday • 1 Corinthians 11:23-34

Q

A

DIGGING DEEPER • The Lord's Supper is not a joke! Yes, we drink out of little cups and eat tiny, little crackers, but we must understand that the Lord's Supper is not about food—it's about Jesus! The church of Corinth evidently had problems taking this seriously, and there are many still today who don't treat the Lord's Supper with the reverence it demands. Let's just briefly summarize the Lord's Supper for anyone who may be unfamiliar with it. It is a special time when Christians gather to remember Jesus' sacrifice by eating bread (which represents His body broken for us) and drinking juice (which represents His shed blood). In doing this, we are obeying Jesus' commandment to remember what He did for us on the cross.

How seriously do you think you should view the Lord's Supper?

friday • 1 Corinthians 12:1-11

DIGGING DEEPER · You are gifted! Really, you are. The Bible says you've been given a gift by the Holy Spirit. He is the One that selects it, and since it's a spiritual gift it is designed to help build the church. Now, ask yourself a question: Do you know what your gift is? Besides our passage today, there are several other lists given in the New Testament (Romans 12; Ephesians 4; 1 Peter 4) that tell us about spiritual gifts. If you're a follower of Christ, you've been given at least one spiritual gift. The Holy Spirit, through the Apostle Paul, wants you to stop being ignorant (v. 1), and find out what your gift is and begin to use it to help others and to help the church grow.
Do you know what your spiritual gift is? How can you use it to help others and glorify God?

saturday • 1 Corinthians 12:12-20

DIGGING DEEPER · You are a part of the body of Christ and you have a role to play within the body. You may only be a knuckle or knee, but you're still a necessary part of the body. You may not be the brain, the heart, or the mouth, but you are still a part of the body. You may only be a small, almost invisible, seemingly unimportant part, but you're still a part of the body and have a role to play within the body. Let me repeat it again, you are part of the body of Christ and you have a role to play within the body! So what are you waiting for? Do your part! Are you functioning the way you should?
What role can you play in your church? Are you currently playing that part or are you just sitting around? What should you be doing this week to be a functioning part of your local church?

The church has been described in all sorts of ways throughout the years, but perhaps the best description of the church is found in 1 Corinthians. The church is a body. It functions best when every part is working with every other part, and is a total failure when one part tries to do it all.

Week 48

prayer focus for this week

sunday • 1 Corinthians 12:21-31

Q
A

DIGGING DEEPER • Aren't you thankful for a digestive system that functions properly, a set of lungs that helps you breathe, and a heart that beats to keep you alive? Even though no one can see your large intestines, lungs, or heart, the truth is they're more important than your eyes, ears, teeth, and hair. If it wasn't for those hidden body parts, you would die. In the body of Christ, there are certainly those members who aren't very prominent as well, and yet they are so important in making sure the body functions properly. Now as to what part of the body you might be, we're not sure, but you have an obligation to function to your maximum potential. Everyone is vitally important. Every member is needed for the church to be successful in glorifying the Lord. Now, go and do it! **What can you do to help your church grow and be healthy?**

monday • 1 Corinthians 13:1-13

DIGGING DEEPER • Love is so important. Without it, it doesn't really matter what you say, how much you know, how much money you give away, or how unselfish you are. While we're talking about how important love is, let's remind ourselves not to water down this word like we're so tempted to do. Let's stop saying, "I love pizza" or "I love basketball," and in the very next breath, talk about how much we love our parents, church, or Savior. Since love is so important, let's get it right. In fact, let's read this passage over, and over, and over again all through our lives. Let's do it until the message finally sinks in, and we really learn to love and have a desire to actively serve others. **After reading this passage, how loving would you say that you are? What can you do today to show your love for others… and the Lord?**

tuesday • 1 Corinthians 14:1-9

DIGGING DEEPER • One of the ways the early church was able to grow so fast was through the spiritual gift of *tongues*. On several occasions throughout the Scriptures (see Acts 2 for an example), we see God's Word communicated by ordinary men to people of other nationalities and languages. Miraculously, God spoke through these ordinary men in a foreign language so that their audience would understand and be able to respond to the Gospel. However, as the church settled in different regions of the world, Paul asked this important question in verse 6, … *if I come unto you speaking with tongues, what shall I profit you…?* It's a good question to ask and one we must continue to ask today. Whatever is spoken should be understood by all who are there. **What if your pastor preached in French this Sunday? Would that be useful?**

wednesday • 1 Corinthians 14:10-17

DIGGING DEEPER • When someone repeats something to you, what are they trying to do? They are attempting to make sure you fully understand what they're saying. If they continue to repeat something over and over again, they want you to fully understand it to such an extent that you will never forget it. This is what Paul seems to be doing as he continues to talk about the subject of the spiritual gift of *tongues*. He wants them to understand the purpose of this gift is not for worship services, where it only causes confusion. In fact, he summarizes by saying, … *I had rather speak five words with my understanding*… than ten thousand in an unknown tongue (v. 19). **In what areas of your life does God continually seem to repeat Himself? What does He want you to more fully understand?**

thursday • 1 Corinthians 14:18-26

DIGGING DEEPER • It's time for you to grow up! Seriously, in some ways, it's time for you to stop being so childish. The Corinthian believers struggled to understand so many spiritual issues because they just weren't very spiritual. Unfortunately, since the time of their conversion, the followers of Christ haven't progressed much. We're still as immature as many of the Corinthian believers. It's time that we grow up! If you've been a Christian for more than a couple of years now, you should be in the process of growing up in the faith. As Paul puts it, *be not children in understanding* (v. 20). So, take off your bib and start reading your Bible. Get out of the high chair and start memorizing some Scripture. Stop having people wait on you and start getting involved in Christian service by helping others. In other words, *grow up!* **Are you becoming more or less like Jesus every day?**

friday • 1 Corinthians 14:27-40

DIGGING DEEPER • God knows what He's doing. He's never confused about what His role is or what He's supposed to be doing. Paul even says, *God is not the author of confusion* (v. 33). While we may be confused, perplexed, or puzzled about various issues in the Scriptures, we can rest assured that it's not God's fault. In fact, the truth is, we've created much of the confusion in our churches ourselves. When we're not creating confusion, Satan himself does all he can to wreak havoc and create confusion. While our churches may not face the same situations the Church of Corinth faced, you can be sure that the enemy will do his best to bring confusion into our lives and into our churches today.
What kind of confusion does Satan bring into churches? How about your church? How about your life?

saturday • 1 Corinthians 15:1-11

DIGGING DEEPER • It's not Easter, but let's say it anyway – Jesus is alive! His resurrection is a vital part of the Gospel which consists of Christ's death, burial, resurrection. The resurrected Jesus was seen by hundreds of people. Isn't that the best news you could hear today and the greatest truth of all time? In fact, just put down your pencil and say aloud, "Jesus is alive" a couple of times. Now some people find it hard to believe that Jesus is alive. However, to have over five hundred eyewitnesses on your side makes a strong case. Not only that, most of those five hundred eyewitnesses died for their belief that Jesus wasn't dead, but indeed alive! So, while it's not Easter, we can still be excited. Why? Because Jesus is alive!
Since you haven't seen Him, why do you believe Jesus is alive today?

No letter lasts forever. While Paul certainly had much more he could have said to the Corinthian believers, he chooses to wrap up his letter with some encouraging news about our future life with Christ. Be ready for some motivational reading.

Week 49

prayer focus for this week

the Question
the Answer

What is the writer saying?

How Can I apply this to my life?

sunday • 1 Corinthians 15:12-19

Q

A

DIGGING DEEPER • If Jesus didn't rise from the dead, then Christianity has a major problem! In fact, if Jesus didn't rise from the dead, then Christianity is pointless, Sundays are pointless, sermons are pointless, and life itself is pointless. Perhaps you've never thought of the resurrection as that important, but it's referred to as one of the cardinal doctrines and is essential to our belief. If you do not believe in Christ's resurrection, then you are not saved. One cannot be a Christian and deny His resurrection. If Jesus didn't rise from the dead, then our sins have not been forgiven, our faith is foolish, and our eternal destiny is certainly not Heaven.

How important is the resurrection? If Jesus wasn't alive, what would that mean for you?

monday • 1 Corinthians 15:20-28

DIGGING DEEPER • Everybody dies. Now that's kind of a morbid way to begin a paragraph, but it's true. We're all going to die. Everybody we know is going to die. Obviously this is very bad news. However, there's some good news. In fact, it's better than good – it's great! Because of what Jesus did for us, we don't stay dead. If we have only been born once (physically), we will die twice (physically and spiritually); but if we've been born twice (physically and the new birth), then we only die once. The truth is, when we close our eyes for the last time in this life, we will open our eyes to a life beyond our wildest imagination; a life with God that will never end. **Aren't you thankful that when you die, you don't stay dead? What would it be like to live without that kind of hope? Do you know someone that is still unsaved?**

tuesday • 1 Corinthians 15:29-38

DIGGING DEEPER • Wake up, come to your senses, and stop living a life of sin! This is the message Paul gives to those in the Church of Corinth who just don't get it. In fact, he goes on to say, *I speak this to your shame* (v. 34). He questions whether they even have a relationship with God. This message is equally relevant today as people everywhere claim the name of Christ, but live in a way that contradicts what He modeled and taught. How can we be so dumb? Let's get out of bed, wipe the sleep out of our eyes, turn our backs on the dead-end path of sin, and follow Christ with everything we've got! **With what specific sins do you struggle? Why haven't you given them up yet? Are you ready to wake up?**

wednesday • 1 Corinthians 15:39-50

DIGGING DEEPER • Have you ever wanted a new body? Maybe you've wanted a muscle-bound body like a body-builder. Maybe you've wanted a model's body that's perfectly proportioned, or an athletic body like your favorite baseball, basketball, or football player. Maybe you're pleased with the body God gave you (as you should be). If you've ever thought about having a different body, you'll be glad to know that one day you will receive a new body and it won't be similar to anything you've ever seen before. It will be a body that never ages, decays, or becomes weary or sick. It will never wear out. More than that, Paul says that our bodies will *bear the image of the heavenly* (v. 49). In other words, we will have an eternal body. Can you say, "Wow?"
What do you think it will be like to never age or get sick again?

thursday • 1 Corinthians 15:51-58

DIGGING DEEPER • Death and sin are powerful. They are two forces no one except Christ has been able to avoid and overcome. However, one day they will be completely abolished and we will be able to say with Paul, *O death, where is thy sting? O grave, where is thy victory* (v. 55)? When Jesus comes back with His Church, death will be defeated and sin will be beaten. They will both be irrelevant at that point. Certainly this is a reason to celebrate and give thanks to God for He has put an end to sin and death by sending His Son, Jesus, to destroy it.
How great will it be for you to finally be removed from the power, penalty, and presence of sin?

friday • 1 Corinthians 16:1-12

Q
A

DIGGING DEEPER • Are you a giver? The Bible indicates that we should be *cheerful* or *hilarious* givers (2 Corinthians 9:7). It's very likely that you don't make a lot of money at this stage in your life, but when you actually do bring home some *bacon*, will you hoard it all for yourself or give some of it back to God? As followers of Christ, we should be known as people who give. In fact, Paul says that those of us who follow Christ should give a certain part of what we've been blessed with back to the Lord. No specific amount is listed, but it is understood that we should give to meet a need. Rather than establishing giving as a habit in your adult years, why not start this habit today? You'll never be able to out give the Lord.
What can you give to the Lord this week?

saturday • 1 Corinthians 16:13-24

Q
A

DIGGING DEEPER • Whenever we finish writing a letter, we always conclude with some sort of friendly ending. We want the recipient to know that everything we've written comes from someone who loves and cares about them. Paul, as he finishes his comments, leaves his readers with several encouraging sentences. He says, *The grace of our Lord Jesus Christ be with you* (v. 23), and then follows that up with, *My love be with you all in Christ Jesus* (v. 24). Although his words have been rough at times, Paul wants his friends in Corinth to know that everything he wrote comes from someone who loves them and wants God's best for their lives.
Who can you encourage today with your words?

Dead Man Talking. Paul is about to be executed for his faith. He has one last book to write and send to one person. One of the godliest men who ever lived writes powerful words of advice. This is the real deal. It's the last letter he ever wrote and is hard core Christianity. Give this study your best! You won't regret it!

prayer focus for this week

the Question
the Answer

What is the writer saying?

How Can I apply this to my life?

sunday • 2 Timothy 1:1-7

Q

A

DIGGING DEEPER • Paul is writing a very personal letter. He is about to die, and there is one last thing he wants to say to his close friend who will keep the ministry going. The last time they were together, they probably parted in tears. That's the last picture Paul has of Timothy. We learn that Timothy was often fearful and timid. Without Paul around, I'm sure Timothy felt like he didn't want to go on—but that's just the opposite of what the Lord empowered him to do. Any *fear* we have about living for God doesn't come from Him. If we trust and obey Him, He can make us incredibly powerful—able to do anything—absolutely anything… even if we feel timid!

What does God want you to do that you are afraid to do? How has God gifted you? Are you using what God has given you for His glory?

monday • 2 Timothy 1:8-12

DIGGING DEEPER · Wouldn't it be great if we were living in Heaven right now? No problems, no sin, no worries, a perfect body, *no fear*. Be honest – don't we all have things that cause us to fear? What if you could actually enjoy some benefits of Heaven now before you're actually there? You can! Paul faced death for following Christ, something we probably haven't had to deal with. Paul knew that death was just a short little bridge to Heaven where he would be with his Savior. If God didn't want him to die—he wouldn't. If he did—he'd be in Heaven. So what is there to fear? God has called us to live a holy life. We need to give Him our best. Enjoy Heaven today!
Do you live out your security in Christ? What should you do to show others you are not ashamed of being a Christian?

tuesday • 2 Timothy 1:13-18

DIGGING DEEPER · Heroes and Zeroes – that is who we read about today. We are introduced to three people. Only one of them was not ashamed of Christ or being connected to Paul. When the rumor got out that Paul was in prison in Rome, Onesiphorus did whatever it took to find him and be an encouragement. We need to realize our responsibility to minister to fellow believers. We should not ignore them when they need our help and support. "What! I'd never do that!" Jesus said, … *as ye have done it unto one of the least of these my brethren, ye have done it unto me* (Matthew 25:40). A day will come when we will need the support of fellow believers. We will reap what we sow.
Do you work hard at supporting fellow believers? Do you know a Christian who often is persecuted (or made fun of) that you could encourage today.

wednesday • 2 Timothy 2:1-7

Q

A

DIGGING DEEPER • *Impossible!* Some of us like the sound of that word because we want to try to do anything that someone says is *impossible*. Others aren't interested in being tricked into trying something they think is too hard. Either way—God is in the business of doing the impossible. The secret is in verse 1 – *Strong in grace!* By ourselves, we aren't very strong, but believing God's grace can empower us to do the impossible… now that's *strong!* That's how to become a *strong* Christian. Part of being strong is never giving up. Verses 3-6 give three illustrations of people who have to work hard and not give up. By God's gracious empowering, you can do anything He wants you to do!
What challenge is there in your Christian walk that seems impossible at the moment? Will you ask God to help you learn about being strong in grace?

thursday • 2 Timothy 2:8-14

Q

A

DIGGING DEEPER • Have you ever missed the chance to witness to someone? You had the opportunity to share about Jesus, and you blew it. Me, too! Witnessing is part of our aim as Christians. Paul, the writer of 2 Timothy, was great at using every opportunity to witness. That's what led to his suffering in prison. However, it was time for Timothy to step up to the plate and be a witness like Paul. Timothy probably missed opportunities, also. That's why verse 13 is so awesome! God's Word can never be held back or chained up. The great news is that God wants to use you! Unfortunately, missionaries and pastors die like everyone else. Who is going to take their place? Who is going to reach your friends now?
Who should you be praying for to receive Christ? Would you focus on sharing Christ with at least one person in the next three days?

friday • 2 Timothy 2:15-19

DIGGING DEEPER • Did you know the Bible is the most widely read book in all of history and around the world today? Amazing? What's even more amazing is the number of people who disagree on what it actually says. That was the problem in today's passage. Verses 16-18 are examples of people who didn't handle God's Word correctly, but verse 15 tells us there's a right way to handle it. Just like in Timothy's day, people today are still trying to distort the Word of God and make it say what they want it to say to suit their own beliefs and behavior. Yes, God's Word can be hard to understand, but you'll never regret studying this book! It's not a school book! It's God's Word! If you desire it enough, He will help you understand it.
Do you ever skip over passages you don't understand? Would you be willing to ask people that can help you? How important is His Word to you?

saturday • 2 Timothy 2:20-26

DIGGING DEEPER • You need to cut through a four-inch board. You have two choices. You can use a brand new stainless steel power saw or a flimsy plastic knife. The choice is easy. But some Christians are about as sharp as a plastic knife for God's glory. We're not pure, clean vessels like verse 20 describes. We're not ready to be used. Verse 22 gives you the plan for staying clean. *Run! Flee! Stay away* from anything that keeps you from being a person God can use for His glory. Perhaps we have Christian friends who aren't so sharp for the Lord. Verses 24-26 show us how to help them. Note the words *kind* and *gentle*.
What sin do you need to run away from? On a scale of 1 to 10, how sharp and ready are you for God? Is there another Christian you can help sharpen?

Paul's life on earth was nearing its end, but we can use his teaching to learn how to live each day! Wait until you reach chapter four. Paul is so brave and focused on Christ that nothing could shake his faith! He wants you to really know the Word of God by: studying it through, praying it in, living it out, and passing it on!

Week 51

the Question
the Answer

What is the writer saying?

How can I apply this to my life?

sunday • 2 Timothy 3:1-7

Q

A

DIGGING DEEPER · What a list! At the top, is the one that describes all the rest—*lovers of their own selves*. Please take note of verse 5! Some of these characteristics might be things we struggle with, but as Christians, we should be changing and growing – always striving to be more like Christ. Perhaps you know of someone described in verses 5 and 7. He may call himself a Christian, but his life doesn't back it up. He pretends to be godly and learning, but certainly isn't. We need to stay away from that person. The question isn't, "Is he a Christian?" rather, "Is he a *growing* Christian by knowing and observing the truth?"

Do any of these characteristics describe you? What are you going to do to change? Who are the Christian friends you should hang out with the most?

monday • 2 Timothy 3:8-12

DIGGING DEEPER • Who wants to live a godly life? (Hopefully, you answered "*Me.*") Now, who wants to be persecuted? Most of us probably wouldn't sign up for that one. Verse 12 makes it clear that the two go hand in hand. Remember this, being persecuted isn't always fun, but it sure beats spending eternity in Hell. Sometimes people make fun of or even hurt us for living for Christ, but He saved us and died for us. We will never regret choosing to follow Him. Look at the end of verse 11. People who do not like us will come and go, but Christ is with us forever! Let's not be swayed by a temporary challenge. Live a godly life! That brings eternal rewards!
Who are you afraid of? Do you want to please man more than you want to please God? Are you looking for God to rescue you from trouble?

tuesday • 2 Timothy 3:13-17

DIGGING DEEPER • Don't you hate it when the fun stops? When a great movie comes to an end, don't you wish it would keep going? Unfortunately, many of us approach our walk with Christ like that—we just stop. We do well for a while, but we stop. That's terrible! Verse 14 was the key for Timothy. *Keep on! Continue! Trust God* to give you the strength to keep going! We find that strength in His Word. How often is our time with God the first thing to go when we get busy or weary of living for Him? When we do that, we unplug ourselves from the power source, and everything goes downhill from there! His Word equips and empowers us for right living (v. 17). Need a charge? Plug in!
If you're struggling in your Christian walk, are you focused on His Word? What are you depending on besides God's Word for strength?

wednesday • 2 Timothy 4:1-4

DIGGING DEEPER • Remember, this is the last chapter of the Bible Paul ever wrote. Of all things he could choose to say to Timothy, Paul says this—*Preach the Word.* Check this out. The word preach here doesn't necessarily mean to *preach* a sermon from the pulpit. It just means *to proclaim*, or *to say out.* This isn't just for Timothy or pastors. It's for all of us. God's Word should penetrate all of our speech. We just can't help but talk about His Word. No matter where, no matter what— just lovingly share God's Word. Yes, there are people who don't want to listen, and that's their choice. We don't force them, but there are plenty of people who do want to hear. Who knows when the fruit will be ripe for harvesting?
Does the Lord often come up in your conversations with people? Commit to sharing one thing from God's Word with someone today.

thursday • 2 Timothy 4:5-8

DIGGING DEEPER • A *drink offering* is a type of sacrifice from the Old Testament. It was something that was set aside for God, and then completely poured out. That's how Paul saw himself. He knew he was going to die, and his life was one that was *poured out* to God for His glory. He didn't waste his time on earth. He did what God wanted him to do. If there is one thing we want to be said of us it is, "They finished well." Paul compares life to a race. We don't know how long our race is, but what would be said if your *race* was over tomorrow? People should be able to look on and say, "He gave Christ his all. He finished well."
Name one area in your life that you could improve. What are you going to do to grow in that area? Would you ask another Christian to help you?

friday • 2 Timothy 4:9-15

Q

A

DIGGING DEEPER • Paul wanted to see Timothy one last time. He told him to come quickly because Paul's execution was not far off. Unfortunately, we learn about Demas here. Demas was a Christian who left Paul to follow his own desires. Wouldn't it be terrible to be known throughout the rest of history as the guy who deserted the Apostle Paul! Unbelievably, there's another one in this passage who also deserted Paul—Mark. It happened in Acts 15. However, we do know that Mark later on must have had a change of heart and pursued Christ. He had really changed. So much so, that Paul wanted to see him again before he died. We all make mistakes, but once again the question is—"How did we finish?"
Have you made a mistake that you haven't corrected yet? Is there a relationship that you need to make right?

saturday • 2 Timothy 4:16-22

Q

A

DIGGING DEEPER • What does it mean to be alone? Maybe you have a job that is boring and there's no one to talk to. Maybe you and your best friend only have one class together in school. What if you had tons of friends, but they never talked to you. Paul is in prison, waiting to be executed, everybody left him, and he's still not alone. For a Christian, being alone is impossible. It might feel like you are all alone, but it's not true. Paul said, *the Lord stood with me, and strengthened me* (v. 17). No, it's not the same as having a real person beside you. It's better! The Lord can protect, comfort, give peace, and love better than anyone else.
Do you pray and spend time in His Word when you are lonely? Would you commit to doing that the next time you feel alone?

If you have ever gotten yourself into a whale-of-a-mess, you won't want to miss this week's reading. Jonah ran from God after being commanded to preach to a people he hated. Later we'll see how Micah was allowed to see seven hundred years into the future and name the exact town in which Jesus would be born.

prayer focus for this week

the Question
the Answer

What is the writer saying?

How Can I apply this to my life?

sunday • Jonah 1:1-17

Q

A

DIGGING DEEPER • Sometimes we have a problem with the way God does things. We may feel like some people should be punished, but God gives them another chance. Obviously, our opinion of others has little to do with God's mercy, compassion, and love. The city of Nineveh in Assyria was notoriously wicked. Because he did not agree with giving Nineveh an opportunity to repent, Jonah deliberately disobeyed God. Great storms follow great disobedience. Jonah found himself in a huge storm! Sometimes we think we know better than God, but this is never the case. The Lord does not force us to obey Him, but He often will arrange our situation to make us wish we had. Three days in the dark, wet, gross, gastric, nasty stomach of a whale would be very persuasive! **Ever tried to run from God? How has God *persuaded* you to obey?**

monday • Jonah 2:1-10

Q

A

DIGGING DEEPER • After suffering the consequences of disobedience, it usually doesn't take us long to pray. Jonah's penitent prayer takes up the whole chapter. He thought he was a goner! We smile when we read it, but it is not funny when it's our bacon in the fire. Jonah said, *"out of the belly of hell cried I ...."* Then he described the awful experience. For three days he flossed his teeth with seaweed. The slimy stuff was wrapped around his head like a turban. He breathed stinking whale's breath. Plankton and saltwater oozed from every orifice of his body. He felt the crushing roller coaster pressure as the whale dove and surfaced. In utter darkness he listened to the moaning, eerie, internal sounds of whales in the deep. He promised to go to the temple, sacrifice, pay tithes... anything... to get OUT!
To get out of trouble, what promises have you made? Have you kept them?

tuesday • Jonah 3:1-10

Q

A

DIGGING DEEPER • It's ironic. Often we don't want God to give another chance to people we think should be judged; but when we are under the heavy hand of judgment, that is precisely what WE want—another chance! If whale vomit (v. 10) smells or looks anything like human vomit, Jonah was a smelly mess! But the grace of God gave him another chance to go to Nineveh and give them another chance. With a seaweed hairdo, dripping plankton goop, every hair on his body bleached white by stomach acid, and whale innards hanging all over him, this preacher's appearance was a sermon in itself. No wonder the king of Nineveh believed the message and proclaimed a fast of repentance. God turned from His fierce anger.
Why is it important to obey the first time? How can our obedience or disobedience affect others?

wednesday • Jonah 4:1-11

Q
A

DIGGING DEEPER • Obeying God, but having a bad attitude does not make points with Him! Jonah preached the warning, but he SO wanted Nineveh to burn. He was well aware of the atrocities of the Assyrians, but he also knew how merciful God is. The Ninevites believed the prophet, and God spared the city. Jonah was *mad*! While waiting on the side of a hill to see what God would do, the Lord caused a gourd to grow overnight and shade the sweltering preacher. Jonah was *glad*. Then God made the gourd wither. Jonah was mad. He wanted to die. When God asked, Jonah snapped back, "*It is right for me to be angry, even to death.*" The prophet was more concerned over a gourd than 120,000 people in need of spiritual birth and faith. God gives compassion and mercy to the worst of sinners.
Have you ever been mad at God? Whose fault was it? Is God's way best?

thursday • Micah 4:1-8; 5:2-4

Q
A

DIGGING DEEPER • "In the last days" indicates the time when the Lord will bring to consummation all the events of human history. Then, Jesus Christ will sit upon the throne of His ancestor, David. He will rule in peace and righteousness. The nations will no longer learn war or make weapons of death and destruction. The King of kings will enforce a literal *Peace on Earth* for one thousand years. The capital of the kingdom will be Mount Zion, which is Jerusalem. This contrasts starkly with the poor state of the Holy City described in Micah 3:12. God's people go through valleys, trials, and even judgment, but the Lord is always watching. He prepares a Deliverer. Micah 5:2 is one of those incredible, detailed prophecies affirming the Bible as authored by God. The town of Jesus' birth is revealed.
How can you defend the Bible as from God? Are we living in the last days?

friday • Micah 6:1-8

DIGGING DEEPER · Have you ever heard someone say, *If only these walls could talk, they would tell the true story?* In God's version He calls on the mountains and the earth as witnesses to the true story of how good He has been to His people. They had forgotten. They had grown tired of religion, giving, faith, service, and sacred things. It was a real problem for the Lord. He gave miracles, deliverances, and provisions, and this is what He got in return. God says, *"O my people, remember,"* (v. 5). In reply (vv. 6-7), it's as if the people say, *WHAT do you want from us? You're not satisfied with thousands of rams and rivers of oil.* As always, outward obedience alone falls far short of what God really wants—*our hearts.* Micah 6:8 proves, not *things,* nor *religion,* but *hearts* are vital with God.
How have you given God your complete heart? Does your behavior match?

saturday • Micah 7:7-20

DIGGING DEEPER · Whenever we return to the Lord after having walked at a guilty distance, we always find Him eager to forgive and willing to restore. After a long period of spiritual decay, prophesies show Israel returning to her God. For a time, enemies will triumph and Jerusalem will be stomped into the mud. Bad times always follow bad decisions that take us away from faithfulness to the Lord. God so loves us and He wants to do greater things for us in the future than He's done in the past (v. 15). Who is a God like our God? He delights in mercy. He does not linger in anger or wrath. He turns with compassion to His people. He casts all our sins into the depths of the sea. God keeps His promises! *"Bless the Lord, O my soul: and all that is within me, bless His holy name"* (Psalm 103:1). Praise God for mercy!
Why is it easy/hard to return to God? How does God deal with our guilt?

241

The following chart is provided to enable everyone using Word of Life Quiet Times to stay on the same passages. This list also aligns with the daily radio broadcasts.

Week 1	Aug 30 – Sep 5	Psalms 77:1-79:13
Week 2	Sep 6 – Sep 12	Psalms 80:1-86:17
Week 3	Sep 13 – Sep 19	Psalms 87:1-91:16
Week 4	Sep 20 – Sep 26	Psalms 92:1-97:12
Week 5	Sep 27 – Oct 3	Psalms 98:1-103:22
Week 6	Oct 4 – Oct 10	Ephesians 1:1-2:22
Week 7	Oct 11 – Oct 17	Ephesians 3:1-4:32
Week 8	Oct 18 – Oct 24	Ephesians 5:1-6:24
Week 9	Oct 25 – Oct 31	Joshua 1:1-5:15
Week 10	Nov 1 – Nov 7	Joshua 6:1-14:15
Week 11	Nov 8 – Nov 14	Joshua 20:1-24:33
Week 12	Nov 15 – Nov 21	Titus 1:1 - Philemon 25
Week 13	Nov 22 – Nov 28	Revelation 1:1-2:29
Week 14	Nov 29 – Dec 5	Revelation 3:1-6:8
Week 15	Dec 6 – Dec 12	Revelation 6:9-10:11
Week 16	Dec 13 – Dec 19	Revelation 11:1-14:7
Week 17	Dec 20 – Dec 26	Revelation 14:8-17:18
Week 18	Dec 27 – Jan 2	Revelation 18:1-20:6
Week 19	Jan 3 – Jan 9	Revelation 20:7-22:21
Week 20	Jan 10 – Jan 16	Judges 2:1-7:25
Week 21	Jan 17 – Jan 23	Judges 8:22-17:6
Week 22	Jan 24 – Jan 30	Amos 1:1 - Obadiah 21
Week 23	Jan 31 – Feb 6	John 1:1-3:12
Week 24	Feb 7 – Feb 13	John 3:13-5:14
Week 25	Feb 14 – Feb 20	John 5:15-6:58
Week 26	Feb 21 – Feb 27	John 6:59-8:24